THE POTENTIAL TRAP:

How to Identify and Live to Your Fullest Capability

By: Mark Benedetti

Copyright © 2021 Mark Benedetti
All rights reserved.
ISBN: 9798586219084

TABLE OF CONTENTS

Introduction 1

Section 1 - Identifying Your Destination

    Chapter 1 - Identifying the Trap..10

    Chapter 2 – What Are Your Skills? 20

    Chapter 3 – What Are Your Passions? 32

    Chapter 4 – Where Do Your Skills Intersect With Your Passions?...42

Section 2 - Determining the Path to Take

    Chapter 5 – Finding a Fit for Your Uniqueness............................52

    Chapter 6 - Refine Yourself...66

    Chapter 7 – Be Daring and Do It...78

Section 3 - Overcoming Speed Bumps and Roadblocks

    Chapter 8 – The Fear Factor...90

    Chapter 9 – The Insecurity Factor...100

    Chapter 10 – The Hesitation Factor..110

Conclusion..120

DEDICATION

To my loving wife.

INTRODUCTION

Have you ever been at a place where you find yourself thinking, "This can't be it."? I've found myself pondering that question a lot lately. I am a 37 year-old married man with 3 kids. I live in a nice house in the suburbs and have a great job that would place me in the upper middle class of America. Yet, there is still something inside of me wanting more. Many people would take inventory of my life and their prognosis of this mindset would be that I am ungrateful, selfish, or greedy. Their prescription to remedy my issue would be, "You need to learn to be content. Why can't you just be grateful for what you have? There are so many people with so much less who would give a kidney to have half of what you've got." I can hear the voices echoing in my head.

But here's the thing, I am grateful. I am content with all the material stuff I have accumulated. My desires for more aren't pointed to having more material possessions, a nicer car, a bigger house, a new wardrobe, or anything like that. It's deeper, much deeper. It is more profound. What makes matters worse is that this feeling isn't going away, in fact it's growing. There are times where I know I've acted or pursued with greed or selfishness in mind. This isn't that. It's not a longing for things; it's a longing for purpose. It's not a longing for money; it's a longing to do something which will resonate beyond just my family.

Full disclosure, I am a Christian. But not in the way some Christians are Christian. A lot of Christians allow their faith to extinguish when they leave the four walls of their church and resume "normal" life. Then, the next Sunday morning, they resume being a Christian for about 80 minutes until the service is over. That's not the type of Christian I am. I'm the type of Christian that believes the Word of God and my beliefs actually impact my thoughts and actions of everyday life. Yes, even after Sunday morning service. So when I read statements in the Bible like, "You will be enriched in every way so that you can always be generous," I am the type of Christian that not only believes what I read but I expect to see it happen. I'm the type of Christian who expects my beliefs to leave the church with me and change my life so that my life reflects my faith. What good is it to believe in something only when you're in the four walls of a church? That's not faith, that's a social club. That's not conviction, that's convenience.

The verse I mentioned in the last paragraph has really challenged my thinking lately. The verse is found in 2 Corinthians 9:11. Let me state it again, "you will be made rich in every way so that you can be generous on every occasion." I've often asked myself the following question which will further illustrate my point,

> "What good is it to believe in something only when you're in the four walls of a church? That's not faith, that's a social club. That's not conviction, that's convenience."

"what would my financial life have to look like for me to be generous on every occasion just like the Bible says?" When I walk past the guy in the Santa hat with the Salvation Army at Christmas. When I hear about someone who lost their job and is having trouble with rent. When there is a feeling in my stomach to pay for someone's groceries behind me at Wal-Mart. Every occasion God? Man, those occasions sure can add up. It seems like there are occasions everywhere we go and everywhere we look. Facebook posts about a GoFundMe for a kid with cancer. #Donate to the most recent natural disaster. That commercial we turn off with the starving children thousands of miles away.

To be generous on every occasion, and I don't mean just throwing in loose change, but to truly make a significant impact through generosity would require a lot of resource. It would take a lot of resource to be able to make a difference in my community for the homeless or the less fortunate. That doesn't mean that we all can't be generous with what resources we currently possess, however, to graduate to the next level of impact will require a graduation to the next level of resource. That next level will take a lot of resource which I do not currently have.

That's why, "this can't be it" has been the song on repeat in my head. Some Christians would say it this way, holy discontent. This is just a spiritual way to say, I know that God has more for my life, and it is frustrating knowing His plan but feeling like I'm on the outside looking in. It is frustrating to know there is something larger for me, but I can't quite see what it is or arrive at the destination. This is a peculiar place to be in as on one hand I am grateful and on the other hand I am reaching for what is next. I had to come to the realization that my career trajectory, as comfortable as it is, does not launch me on a path to see that kind of resource the Bible mentions.

So, what has to happen, or change, or start in order to live the life the Bible promises? I'll admit, my life, as it stands right now, is extremely blessed. However, financially, I am not nearly in the place where we have more resource than needs around us. So, I must conclude that there is a God designed plan to change my trajectory so that I can be truly generous on every occasion. I must also conclude that this belief does not qualify me as greedy or discontented but motivated to discover and do the plan that God designed specifically for me.

> "You're not where you want to be yet, but you're also not where you used to be."

SETTING A DESTINATION

One thing I love to move towards is a vacation. Who doesn't? If you don't enjoy vacationing, then I doubt we could be friends. As a family we usually take one week of vacation together a year. We usually go to a beach in South Carolina with my family or my wife's family. Some years we are lucky enough to take two vacations in one summer. What I've learned about myself as we have gone on about two dozen of these beach vacations over 13 years of marriage is that I am a destination driven person. Meaning, I enjoy setting a destination, planning for the destination, packing for the destination, and arriving at the destination. Notice I left out a very important part. A part that is essential for any vacation to take place. Without this one part no vacation could have ever happened or will ever happen (except for a 'staycation' which I'd argue is no vacation at all). That one part is the process of traveling. Traveling is when you are in-between two locations. You're not where you want to be yet, but you're also not where you used to be. Traveling is tough. Traveling is uncomfortable. Traveling can be dangerous. Traveling will test you and frustrate you. So, I guess my "holy discontent" could also be described as traveler's fatigue.

I know I'm not at the destination in my journey with God, but I'm also not where I used to be either. I'm somewhere in the middle. From where I sit in my suburban kitchen, the "generous on every occasion" type of life sure does seem far away but with hindsight I can look backwards to see how far I've already come. I've got a long way to go and a lot of traveling still ahead which can be both exciting and intimidating. But I've already come so far which makes me grateful and confident.

The book of Exodus tells the story of a nation called Israel who were miraculously delivered from over 400 years of slavery by God through the leadership of Moses. After much deliberation and some amazing miracles, the pharaoh of Egypt released the Israelites from slavery and declared them free people.

> "My mission is to arrive at the destination. As a result, all my actions support my mission."

As they leave the country of Egypt there is a journey they must take to a special land God handpicked for them. Many theologians believe the entire Israelite nation, of approximately two to three million people, could have made this journey in about 11 days. The problem was that they were terrible at traveling. Horrible. I'm sure you know some people that are terrible travelers. Maybe you are a bad traveler. There are some people I refuse to travel with in caravans. I won't name names, even if some of these people are my immediate family members. See, when I travel, I don't stop except for gas, breakfast and one or two (maximum) bathroom breaks. My kids are given small rations of water because if only a bit goes in, then not much can come out. It is amazing how few bathroom breaks you need when you drink 1 ounce of water per every hour. Also, I don't take the scenic route, but always take the shortest distance. I'll gladly pay tolls. Why? My mission is not to be in a car. My mission is to arrive at the destination. As a result, all my actions support my mission. My decisions to restrict water aren't to be unnecessarily cruel to my kids, the decision supports the mission. All my decisions support my mission of arriving at the destination as quick as possible.

The Israelites found traveling to be very frustrating. Their frustration then boiled over into complaining. As a result of their complaining they turned an 11-day scenic tour into a 40-year epic saga. This prolonged journey ended up defining many of these people as they lost their sense of the destination and became wanderers. They lost sight of the vision and mission at hand. They lost sight of the fact that they weren't supposed to take up permanent residence in the desert. They were only passing through. Because they lost sight of the mission then their actions seemed to lack purpose and value.

God had a specific destination for the Israelite people. At the specific destination each family would have encountered their place in the culture. Some would become hunters, soldiers or blacksmiths. Some would be priests, work construction, or make clothes. Each person would fulfill a plan or purpose for their life. They would have stopped traveling and began contributing if they just could have arrived. They weren't destined to wander; they were destined for a destination. At the destination they would have stopped wandering and began producing to fulfill their purpose.

I just heard today that an author was traveling through the United States and interviewed people from all over the country randomly on the streets. He asked one question, "what is your number one fear?" The question wasn't, "what is something you're afraid of?" But instead, what is the one thing you fear the most. The most common answer wasn't spiders, or public speaking, or even death. The response he heard the most was a fear of having a meaningless life and to die with untapped potential. Wow. What a terrible thought. To die after living a meaningless life. I would have guessed people were afraid of death or being alone, living without being loved, having to bury a child or something even more tragic. The results of his survey were shocking to me. I realized when I heard the results of this survey that many others were having the same traveler's fatigue, holy discontent, and asking the same questions I was asking.

> "...the danger lies within self-defining who we are and then living to that inherently limited potential."

FILLING IN YOUR BLANK

A terrible trap of modern western culture is how self-definition has infiltrated our mindsets. I am a _____. We fill in the blank on the name tag of our own lives. We do this when we meet new people in social settings, "Hi, my name is Mark and I'm an accountant." Blank filled in and self-definition defined. "I'm a teacher." It's what we do to get to know new friends and provide some foundation in understanding a person's background. The simple response is often harmless and innocuous; however, the danger lies within self-defining who we are and then living to that inherently limited potential. So, in essence, what we say is I am an accountant and so my future potential lies within the box of all the things an accountant can do or could do. See the trap now?

So how do we escape from this trap? That is a question I have been asking myself lately. The first step is to identify that the trap even exists. What's worse is that it's a trap we build ourselves, we then set the trap and fall right into it. It's almost like a plot for a Three Stooges episode. As children who have hopes and dreams, we grow up with aspirations and potential. Then, through life experiences, expectations of others, and patterns we observe, the vast majority of society falls into the self-definition trap.

Personally, the Bible is my favorite tool in my utility belt of life. It inspires. It guides. It stabilizes. These are some of the reasons why I love reading it. It's filled with stories and principles that blow up the thought processes entrapping our minds. The Bible tells me that God has a plan for my life and that His plan for my life is greater than anything I could ever imagine. What God tells us is that our imagination doesn't compare to what He can and wants to do. Let me tell you, I have a wild imagination. Don't believe me? Ask my wife, I can conjure up some wild stuff. But to know that God has a plan for me, not just humanity in general, but a unique and specific plan for Mark Samuel Benedetti. It encourages me. It's like nitro boost when I feel weary from traveling between destinations. It energizes me to keep moving forward to live in the purpose for which I was created.

> "We aren't limited to this OR that, but we can be this AND that."

I am learning that the first step towards the destination, towards purpose, is to free ourselves from this trap like the Israelites needing freed from slavery. Our mindset regarding our future needs to detach from our past, our family history, and our own brain's limitations, and instead attach to what God says about us. God says that as high as the heavens are above the earth, that's the grandeur of His plans for us.

Instead of living trapped to one thing, one job, one career, one self-definition; we need to embrace being multiple. I'm not talking about cloning or having multiple personalities. What I mean is an understanding that we can be multiple things. We aren't limited to this OR that, but we can be this AND that.

I've always lived in, or around, Pittsburgh. As a result, I love the Steelers (or as it's pronounced in Pittsburgh...the Stillers). When I was in middle school the Steelers drafted a young quarterback from the University of Colorado named Kordell Stewart. He played quarterback in college but because of his unique skill set he was able to play various positions for the Steelers instead of just quarterback. In his rookie year he developed the nickname, "Slash" because he wasn't just used as a quarterback. He was used as a quarterback/running back/wide receiver/punt returner. He couldn't be labeled by just one position or just one thing. Thus, he was given the unique slash status. This is not something that happens only in professional sports as others have followed in Kordell's footsteps outside of the sports world.

I have been caught up in the wave of podcasts over the past few months. I've eschewed the habit of listening to music or sports talk to use my time in the car to learn something. I recently listened to a podcast where Elon Musk was interviewed for two and a half hours. Over the course of 150 minutes of discussion, Elon Musk discussed a wide array of topics. One topic included all the different endeavors Elon has started or is currently deeply involved. This list includes electric vehicles, spaceships, transportation tunnels, artificial intelligence, solar roofs, and flame throwers to name a few. He is most definitely a "slash". He stated that the only limitation to his creative ability are the 24 hours in each day. His ideas to solve problems he sees are endless but the hours in a day are not.

What a refreshing stance on the potential of mankind! Whether Elon believes in God or not, his belief on his potential certainly aligns with what the Word of God says on the subject. Because of his intellect, background, creative ability, and work ethic he will not limit himself or his future by just doing one thing. Does that make him greedy or lacking contentedness? Not necessarily. To me it illustrates the possibility of living a life without a preconceived notion of limits. My past doesn't define me, my potential does. My LinkedIn account isn't the best indicator of my future, my imagination determines my fate.

MY "/"

I believe that God has made each of us with a slash in mind. We shouldn't be labeled by one finite definition because then we can only produce from one finite source. We see this in the Bible with King David. David was a ferocious warrior / skilled musician / eloquent song writer / diligent shepherd / beloved king /

husband / father. From the wide variety of skills and passions, King David was able to produce valuable services for his nation and generate great wealth and influence. If he only focused on his music, he would have never killed Goliath. If he only focused on fighting, he wouldn't have written the book of Psalms. If he only focused on being a shepherd, he would have never become king. I wonder how many potential kings have ignored an opportunity to leave the sheep and step into a kingdom. I wonder how many people are living in a pasture when they should be in a palace.

WHAT'S NEXT?

So how do we determine what will be the description after our next '/'. Most of us have the first describer locked down. You're a salesperson or electrician or manager in manufacturing. But what's next? That's what this book is about, how to determine what might be next for you. Not that I can tell you what you should do next, but I believe some simple questions and serious introspection can help you self-discover what the next thing for you might be.

So, what is stopping you? What is stopping me? Is it the comfort of what we have or can do? Is it a fear of failing or wasting years? Let's ditch this way of thinking and move forward. What mindsets beset our parents or grandparents don't need to carry forward inside of us. Let's add some slashes to our business cards. Let's become multiple; multiple skilled, multiple talented and multiple minded.

SECTION 1 – DEFINING THE POTENTIAL TRAP

CHAPTER 1 – IDENTIFYING THE TRAP

About three or four years into my accounting career I was working for a public accounting firm in downtown Pittsburgh. I was a senior accountant at the time and was beginning to attend networking events as a way to generate referrals and hopefully bring new business to the firm. Most of these events consisted of a bunch of accountants, bankers, and lawyers in some room pretending to be interested in each other's area of expertise. Wow, how boring does that sound? I'm falling asleep just typing it out.

Anyways, I did make a contact with a lawyer and my wife and I were invited to a Pittsburgh Pirates baseball game with my new contact and her husband. So, we went one summer night to network and enjoy a free baseball game. It didn't hurt that the law firm's tickets were in this awesome private box with all-you-can-eat food. So, over the course of 9 innings, and a lot of nachos (I mean, a lot!), we talked a bit about business but mostly it was small talk. Where do you live? How did you meet? Where did you go to high school and college? Stuff like that. What we came to find out was not only was my contact a lawyer at a large, prestigious law firm but her husband was a doctor. Not only was he a doctor, but he was one of the team doctors that worked with the Pittsburgh Pirates. It gets better, not only did he work with professional athletes, but he had his own practice. The kicker was that he was only a few years older than me.

Yikes. This power couple, a doctor and a lawyer, were very impressive. On the surface they had it all complete with an incredible sounding home in a wealthy suburban community near Pittsburgh. They had prestige, money, and youth all at once. They traveled extensively, when they weren't working, and had all the material things most people seek in clothes, cars, boats, jewelry, and everything else you could want.

We walked away from that evening laughing about how we must have looked to them as a lowly accountant and teacher. If they were a high-powered couple, then we were a low-powered couple. If they were a nuclear power plant, then we were a few 9-volt batteries. What was interesting was we weren't insecure about what we did or jealous of the other couple. It was a situation where we were laughing at how different we felt economically. This other couple, the power couple, were really nice people. They weren't arrogant or stuck-up. They didn't flaunt their affluence over us. They didn't insult or belittle our chosen careers. As I reflect on that night the most interesting part was what we said about ourselves afterward. The other couple wasn't belittling us, in fact, we were belittling ourselves. Everything we felt came from one place, our own thoughts. They didn't project those thoughts on us, our own minds were doing all the work for us.

THE TRAP DEFINED

What I came to realize after this encounter is that our own minds were working overtime, not to just present the facts or process the new relationship, our own minds were working to define us. Working to define our influence as negligible. Working to define our significance as already maximized. Working to define our potential as limited. I can still remember the voice in my head:

> "You're just an accountant who knows accountant things and does what accountants do. Your wife is just a teacher who teaches little kids. Now, drive home in your pathetic 2001 Chevy Cavalier."

What a trap. What a con.

I call it the Potential Trap. It's a way of thinking with the goal of trapping our full potential inside a mindset filled with false limitations. The Potential Trap isn't a new thing. It's been around hundreds and hundreds of years.

In the Bible, a few chapters after the Israelites had finally arrived at their destination, the book of Joshua tells us that God instructed the leaders to send twelve spies into this new land to see what it was like. They were to explore the land to learn about the terrain, to see if it was fruitful or barren, and to see what kind of people were currently living and occupying this land. After forty days of espionage behind enemy lines, the twelve spies all returned and began telling the rest of their countrymen how awesome this territory was. They described how it was fruitful and brought back samples of huge grapes. They described how beautiful the land was with rivers and valleys. But there was one problem with this new land, in fact, it was a big problem. Giants. It was inhabited by giants. Literally, giant men who would most assuredly be difficult to conquer when it came time for a battle. They made an interesting statement about themselves during their report regarding the giants. They said, "We were like grasshoppers next to them and that's what they thought too." What's interesting is the Israelites were only assuming that is how the giants were perceiving them. It doesn't say, "We were like grasshoppers next to them and that's what they said." The story says, "That's what they thought too." How did they know their internal thoughts? Their own minds were telling them that. It was the Potential Trap.

> "What you do is not who you are."

Their minds told them, "You're a grasshopper." The brain received the signal and so that is what they became. Grasshoppers. They thought small so they believed they were small. Their small beliefs made them act small. Their small actions ultimately resulted in them living small. Thinking a certain way will lead to believing a certain way. Believing will lead to acting and acting will lead to living a certain way. But if this way of negative thinking can lead us towards a negative result then isn't the opposite also true? Thinking big will lead to believing big which will lead to acting big and living big.

What you do is not who you are. It's so very important that it bears repeating.

"What you do is not who you are."

A simple statement to recalibrate our minds and how we think. Our thoughts are extremely powerful and often underestimated. If you want to take control of your future, you must first take control of your mind. You, and only you, must control your own mind and thoughts. Others can encourage us and inspire us, but the change has to occur from within for it to take root.

When I read stories like this one about Joshua and the other spies, I feel encouraged to expand and broaden the way I think about myself. This story also serves as a warning of the power that small-minded thinking can impose on our future. So, now I want to pay forward the encouragement that I have already received. I want to encourage you to redefine yourself. Don't allow your past, or your present, to dictate your future. Listen, it's your brain, you can control it. Your brain doesn't work for someone else. Your brain doesn't work for your family members, your culture, your past or the people in your life telling you that you can't do something.

> "...what you do cannot define you unless YOU allow it."

There are a lot of different ways and different sources by which our minds receive votes on who we are. Our past submits a vote that we crack under pressure based on a high school homecoming football game. Our family submits a vote that college is out of reach because no one in the family has ever attended a four-year institution. Our employer submits a vote that we'll be stuck in our current position forever. Our culture tells us that that we are good, but not special or unique, and we should settle for good because good is good enough. But here's the truth, those outside influences are merely that, influences. They might try to persuade your mind towards thinking a certain way about your yourself but ultimately you, and you alone, have the final say.

What you do for a living does not have the right to define who you are. In fact, what you do cannot define you unless YOU allow it. This isn't a new concept. In fact, when you Google the phrase of "what you do is not who you are", there are a lot of people who have said very similar messages. However, I would assert that the Potential Trap coined the phrase ever since mankind has assumed singular positions within our societies. I have heard this phrase many times over in my head since graduating college.

> You are an accountant. You'll always be an accountant. You can excel within that field but don't venture outside of the world of accountancy. Those unknown waters of entrepreneurship look awful choppy and unpredictable. Many intelligent, driven, and well-funded people have drowned in those treacherous waters. Just stay in your lane. You're an accountant.

Eventually, as we entertain our own personal potential traps long enough the reasons to stay trapped seem reasonable and logical. I like to say it this way, "Anything you allow to define you will confine you." What does that mean? Well, it means that the definitions we allow to describe who we are, what we do, and what we are capable of will create a space for us to live in within the boundaries of those definitions.

> The Trap: You're not a risk taker.

> Our Response: Well, that's true. I'm not a big risk taker.

If we accept the self-definition of "not a risk taker", we limit ourselves by eliminating the chance of doing anything associated with risk. This limits us in our careers, relationships, personal finances, and even our faith.

Over time we develop this weird trust with our own personal Potential Trap. We oddly begin to trust our Potential Trap's judgement for what is best for our lives. We oddly begin to trust in the traps assessment of our personality, character and potential. This is where it gets dangerous and damaging. The trap actually feels safe and comfortable. This is the moment when our DEFCON alarm system should be going off like a nuclear warhead was just launched at your house and signaling something has gone terribly wrong.

> The Trap: Accountants are boring and uninteresting. Who wants to read a book written by an accountant? People won't be able to stay awake past the introduction.

> My response: Thought rejected.

OUR POTENTIAL RE-DEFINED

But here's the thing, I am not boring at all; ask my wife. In fact, I know a lot of accountants and many of them aren't boring either. My wife has to continually pull me out of friends' houses to leave when we are having a good time because she is tired and wants to sleep. I love being around other people. I'll admit it, I like being the center of attention. I love to make people laugh and act 10+ years younger than my age. In fact, the only thing that makes me an accountant is a degree on my wall and a certificate from my passed CPA exam.

You might, and hopefully do, refer this book to a friend. "I just read this book called *The Potential Trap* written by this accountant from Pittsburgh." An accountant who wrote a book. Even I have had to redefine how I refer to myself so that the statement of "an accountant who wrote a book" is incorrect. I would also suggest that "an author who does accounting" wouldn't be correct either. I'm not an accountant that wrote a book, nor am I an author who knows accounting. I am an outgoing, energetic person who launches people into their potential, who believes that the future isn't predetermined, who has ideas and creativity, and who also knows a good deal about accounting. Now, I don't see myself as one thing. Now I am beginning to see that a lot of slashes are required to fully describe me. Do you see all the slashes in that last comment?

Inspirer/Teacher/Accountant/Student/Leader/Entrepreneur/Husband/Author/Father/Speaker

I'm a slasher and I'm proud of it. My slashes don't define me, they describe me. See the difference. When you embrace the '/' you embrace the opportunity to not be limited. The only thing between you and the next phase of your life is a slash. /. One simple line leaning slightly to the right. That slash isn't on your keyboard just for web addresses. It's there to prod you into the next stage of your life. No more wandering around a desert, no more meandering through life, no more traveler's fatigue. Now it's time to embrace who you are and fulfill the purpose with which God destined you to fulfill.

You are always in control of two things in your life, your thoughts and your words. Always, always, always. No one can force to you think a certain way and no one can force you to speak a certain way. I've found that controlling these two important areas, our thought life and our words, make all the difference in the world in determining if we identify and destroy the potential trap set against our future.

CONTROLLING OUR THOUGHTS

So, how do we control our thoughts and words? Let's talk about our thought life first.

I want to encourage you to set in your mind a pattern of thinking bigger when it comes to you, your future, your potential and your abilities. My wife and I recently made a vision board which hangs in our bedroom. We pinned pictures to our cork board and created a vision before our eyes of things we want to see happen with ourselves, our family, our finances, our careers, our bank account, our house, etc. We had to have a vision for our thoughts to have a direction. The Israelites couldn't stop complaining in the desert because they lost the vision of what they were doing, traveling. I've heard it said, "you will become what you behold." The vision board we created was an instrument to ensure we were consistently beholding something we wanted to become. We are consistently letting our eyes behold a vision of what we want our future to look like.

A clear vision provides a clear direction. The Bible says in Proverbs 29:18, "Where there is no vision, people perish." Each one of us needs to clearly set forth a vision to give a structure to our actions. Like I mentioned earlier when describing how I travel, all my actions support the mission or vision. My goal is to arrive quickly, so my actions support that vision. We end up as aimless wanderers when our actions aren't building towards anything that has been defined. It would be like building a house with no blueprint or plan. The house would not function properly if plumbing wasn't installed to the bathrooms or kitchen.

So, why are we thoughtful when it comes to building a house, but we give no thought towards how we are building our life? It's time to lay out a blueprint for our future. It's time to hit the reset button on how our thoughts incarcerate our potential by defining our abilities as limited or insufficient. We have to have a vision for our

"A clear vision provides a clear direction."

own lives. George Washington Carver said, "Where there is no vision, there is no hope." Vision is important. I don't want to live without hope and I certainly don't want to perish, so I must clearly identify and passionately pursue the vision I have for my life. Our thought life then must support the defined vision. At times you must force your thoughts to be supportive. I promise you, at times, you might feel frustrated or dejected at the rate of change you are seeing manifest. But don't give up mentally and don't allow yourself to quit on seeing your visions become reality.

CONTROLLING OUR WORDS

Next, let's talk about how important and critical our words are to realizing our full potential. Words are like building blocks. Words take the vision from the mind and begin building whatever is spoken. If we use negative words to describe ourselves then we build negative and restricting situations. If our words are positive and growth focused, then we build positive situations. Negative vocabulary builds a prison that incarcerates us within a prison wall of words. Ultimately, negative words build destruction situations while constructive words build constructive results.

Once a vision for your future is created then <u>only</u> speak words which support that vision. Once you have controlled your thought life then only speak about yourself, your potential, and your future in an affirming manner. The Bible tells us in Proverbs 18:21 that, "the power of life and death is in your tongues and you will eat the fruit of your own words." Even people in the secular world have learned how important our words are. A quick search on Google will provide thousands of links to websites, book, articles, and videos of people in all faiths that practice this lifestyle mentioned in the Bible. Think of it this way, today you are eating the fruit of the words you spoke yesterday. Does it taste good? Are you eating sour grapes or ripe ones? Quit saying that you're stupid. Stupid tastes bad. Quit saying you're a failure. Failure tastes old. Quit saying you'll never do anything because then you never will. Instead, make a choice today to only speak in an affirming, positive manner when referencing yourself, your future, and your potential.

Now that we have a correct vision and are supporting our vision with our words, how do we determine what to do next? This is where my personal frustration was mounting. I had a correct thought life, my words were supporting my vision, but I didn't know what to do next. Remember how I talked in the introduction about traveling, that's the frustrating place that led me to my laptop to begin writing. So, how do you find the outlet for your frustration?

FINDING THE UNIQUE

Let's apply this in a practical way. How do we determine what is after our next slash? How do we identify what is best for us to do next? There is one word painted on the starting line of your next idea, business or venture. That word is uniqueness. Meaning, the vehicle to take you from where you are at currently to your unlimited, God-inspired, full of slashes potential, is the uniqueness found on the inside of you. Your uniqueness has extreme value. Your uniqueness is where you will find your purpose in life. Your uniqueness has an unbelievable amount of potential to take you somewhere you never could have imagined.

Uniqueness.

Uniqueness kind of has a cheesy connotation to it. Doesn't it? I have this image of a kindergarten teacher telling a bunch of five-year-old kids how super-duper-extra wonderful they are while snot runs down their cheeks. Sometimes uniqueness is used as a polite way of calling someone weird. "Did you meet Mary from HR?" "Yea, she sure is unique." Uniqueness isn't just to describe someone who is a weirdo or has a few screws loose. Each and every one of us has a unique blend of personality, skills, background, perspective, passion, and creativity which when cultivated can bring some new into this world. Never seen before, that is a phrase that describes you and what is inside of you. And I mean that in a good way too!

I am unique. So are you.

Have you ever been driving down the road and almost wrecked your normal-person car staring at another car? Maybe a Lamborghini or Ferrari passes you and it catches your eye. Why is that? The uniqueness of that car draws your attention and focus. What is interesting is the uniqueness of the car is so intense that we actually forget we are driving a giant machine with humans inside and lose focus, putting ourselves into danger, to stare at something else. The rareness of that vehicle consumes your eyes. Your gaze is drawn towards it.

> "Each and every one of us has a unique blend of personality, skills, background, perspective, passion, and creativity which when cultivated can bring some new into this world."

Why? Because most of us don't often see these types of exotic cars on the road, and because the car is unique, we give it our attention. Our attention increases its value.

   The same thing goes for a person who is living in their uniqueness. These are people that often draw our attention, our focus and thus we increase THEIR value. Think of famous athletes like Christiano Ronaldo, Michael Jordan, Tom Brady or Sidney Crosby. These four are loved by many fans, hated by many opponents' fans, but respected by almost all fans. Why? Each one found what he was uniquely gifted and skilled to do and then pursued that endeavor with all his passion and heart. They are unique and they showcase their uniqueness for the world to see. Guess what? The world pays top dollar to watch these men live in their uniqueness.

Good isn't good enough. Average isn't acceptable any longer. In fact, good sucks. Average is awful and normal is an insult. My wife and I aren't just your standard accountant and teacher. We will be more. We are more and we refuse to settle for anything less.

I've found that discovering our own uniqueness isn't cheesy or lame at all. In fact, it's one of the more profound, informative and adult things I've done. It's not terribly hard to do or difficult to comprehend. In fact, I think it can be accomplished with asking ourselves three simple questions discussed in the following chapters.

CHAPTER 2 – WHAT ARE YOUR SKILLS?

I was born in 1983. Some studies would say I am a very young Generation X'er, while others say I'm a very old Millennial. Whichever generation I'm officially a part of, I know what my particular generation was told as children: "When you grow up you can be whatever you want to be. You could be an astronaut, a Broadway dancer, an NFL quarterback or even the President of the United States of America." Do you want to know my take? What a load of garbage. I can assure you; I could not be many of those things, especially a Broadway dancer or an NFL quarterback. My rhythm is less than perfect, and my body could not withstand even a single hit from an NFL linebacker.

There are a number of professions in this world that require very specific and elite physical gifts and abilities like professional sports. We are either born with these traits or we are not. I played a few years of Division 3 college soccer. I promise you, professional soccer in Europe was not in the cards for me. I trained very hard for soccer. I practiced very hard at it as well. I received great coaching, but there was a limit on my athletic ability which was set at birth. This isn't specific to just sports either. There are other professions that require an elite aptitude for math and sciences. If you want to be a great structural engineer or even a fighter pilot, then you'd better love and be great at math. Other professions in the arts or design require an ability to think creatively and visualize an end product before it exists. Some people are born with this ability and some are not. My wife is very visual and creative. She was born with, and then further honed, her creative eye. I am not very creative. She can do things that I can't. She has gifts and talents, and so do I, just different ones.

You can't be whatever you want to be. Neither can the rest of us. I know that sounds really discouraging and the opposite of what we are supposed to teach our children, however, it doesn't make it less true. The question of, "what do I want to be?" should be deleted from our brains. Rather what we should be asking is, "what direction are my skills pointing me towards?"

I will most assuredly be parenting my children and guiding them towards their careers through the lens of their skills AND their desires, not solely their desires alone. If my daughter is a mediocre athlete, then I will guide her away from athletics and towards something that she actually does excel in doing. I'm not trying to squash her dreams. I'm not trying to be a horrible parent. In fact, I believe that letting her walk down a path that will eventually lead her towards let down would be even worse. I am trying to set a course of success for her to begin walking down as early as young adulthood. If my son doesn't have a natural aptitude towards math and analytical thinking, then maybe accounting and finance aren't for him. The same logic that we would engage to counsel our children or a freshman in college should be the same logic we apply to our own lives.

> "Rather what we should be asking is, "What direction are my skills pointing me towards?"

THE FIRST QUESTION

The first step towards setting a new direction is taking an honest assessment of ourselves. We have to take inventory of our lives and it starts now. So, let me pose the first question to ask in order to break free from the Potential Trap.

The first question is:

What are my skills?

This question is the starting place of discovering what good or service we could potentially offer. This question does not ask, "what am I currently doing?" Or even, "what is my current job?" It's bigger than those answers.

> What am I actually skilled at? What am I good at? What am I trained to do? What have I developed in myself that I do better than most people?

Begin to think about your skills in a broader sense. Think outside of just merely tasks, previous jobs, and concrete skills and be sure to consider some of the softer skills as well. Soft skills like listening, public speaking, motivating, encouraging, being funny or hospitable. Are you creative? Do you think outside the box? Are you good at solving problems? These soft skills are equally as important to consider in order to generate a complete listing of what we do better than most other people.

Ask yourself:

> What do you bring to the table? Are you outgoing and gregarious? Are you thoughtful and considerate? Are you great with your hands and can build or repair seemingly anything? Do you have an advanced degree in mathematics? What do you love to do outside of your day job? Does anyone ever tell you that you should sell your pies or homemade clothes? Are you the life of the party? Are you good at discerning people's intentions or motivations?

I hope these questions are prompting you to view the entirety of the skills that you have developed as just that, skills. Too often our human nature is to significantly underestimate our own abilities. I think it's because what we do is so common to us that it robs us of seeing the value we possess. We go to our jobs every day, and since it might be easy or natural to us, we assume that other people wouldn't value what we have to offer. Just because you don't get nervous speaking to a group doesn't mean that other people feel the same way. Just because you understand how different ingredients mix well together doesn't mean that other people have any clue of how to bake.

Don't label a skill as nonexistent just because you might have deemed it to be insignificant. Let me repeat, don't ignore a skill because to you that ability doesn't seem to be very valuable or unique.

You might be great at making people laugh and your friends love being around you because of how much fun they have with you. Don't ignore that, it's a skill. Not everybody possesses that ability which means it's something you can provide which others cannot. Did you know Bob Newhart was an accountant before he launched into his comedy career? I wonder if anyone tried to discourage him during his unique career change. At some point, he had to identify that he was particularly skilled at making people laugh with his dry sense of humor.

It's important to understand that fulfilling your future potential might involve a skill you possess that you're not currently utilizing at its fullest capacity. There are other stories of Famous Amos and Colonel Sanders who were both really good at making a few things in the kitchen. This allowed them to sell their specific food to an entire nation. It didn't matter how good of a hamburger Colonel Sanders could make; his specialty was fried chicken. Likewise, it didn't matter how Famous Amos's muffins tasted because of how good his cookies tasted. The important thing in this step is to isolate what skills you possess. It doesn't matter how obvious or innocuous. It doesn't matter if you developed them slowly over years or were born with a talent.

"Don't label a skill as nonexistent just because you might have deemed it to be insignificant."

IDENTIFYING SKILLS

I love my wife. She is extremely industrious. She has an entrepreneurial mind and spirit about her which is always generating new ideas. Actually, I owe all of my entrepreneurial aspirations to her and her example. Not only is she entrepreneurial, which is a great starting point, but she is creative and crafty. Not crafty in a burglar sort of way, but crafty in a Joann Fabrics, Hobby Lobby sort of way. When we had our first daughter, she developed a horrible habit (Some would call it an obsession or disease. Not me, but some people might.) of buying hand-made boutique dresses for our daughter to wear. These dresses were adorable, and I must admit she did look very cute in them. However, if my description of "hand-made boutique dress" wasn't a big enough clue, then let me be frank they were expensive. Like, $60 plus shipping per dress expensive. I abruptly and judicially put the "kibosh" on this dress epidemic.

So, my wife starts inspecting these dresses and looking up patterns online. She bought some fabric from Hobby Lobby, studied patterns, pulled out an old sewing machine and asked for advice. Within a few days she started making her own. Now, instead of paying $60 per dress she was making them for less than $6 per dress. She posted a few pictures of Madi wearing her new hand-made, non-boutique, dress on Facebook and the compliments came flooding into her comments section. Soon the compliments turned into order requests. "I love that dress. My daughter is a size 5. Can you make her one?" Within a few weeks my wife had her very own online boutique receiving dozens of requests per month making hundreds of dollars per month.

I knew things were getting serious when we went to Hobby Lobby one day for her to buy more fabric. It was like we owned the place when we walked into store. "Hi Amy! How are you? Here for more fabric? This must be your husband. Did your daughter have a good check up at the doctors?" I had to pull my wife aside and find out just how much these people knew about our lives. After a few months she was spending hours per day sewing these dresses. My job was to take these packages to the post office on my lunch break. Some days it would be four to five packages being sent all over the country. North Carolina, Utah, and New Mexico would all be in the same day. Now, should I take the credit for this little business? Sure, why not!?! It was my frugal nature that forced her hand towards creating instead of purchasing.

> "A skill left unidentified is a resource left unmined."

A skill left unidentified is a resource left unmined. If my wife would have doubted herself, or denied her own ability, then the resources we received from those dresses would never have been realized. Those resources would have remained undiscovered and unmined.

This wasn't the only time she took it upon herself to create instead of purchase. It happened a few years later as she was making jewelry in our bedroom. She bought a necklace from a jewelry party. After inspecting it and some internet research she concluded, "I could easily make this necklace with these materials and some tools." It was the same exact process as her hand-made dresses, just with a different resource. Instead of fabric it was crystals.

What this taught me is that the resource being used is not as important as the skill being used. Do you see the pattern? She applies her skill of creation with whatever resource (clothes, jewelry) in order to create value. The skill is her eye to see an opportunity to utilize her creativity and then applying her entrepreneurial spirit. Skill meets resource and creates value. The resources being used is the variable in this equation. The resource is what changes. Her true skill remains the common denominator regardless of its application. What resource is waiting for you to dig it up and utilize it? I wonder what resources are right under your feet waiting for your skill to engage with it so that it can impact your life? Allow your skills to be the tools that unearth the value all around you.

Another mistake could be if you overestimate your abilities or skills in a particular area. I love to golf. As I type this sentence my official GHIN handicap is 4.2, real golfers know what that means. If you're not a golfer let me translate, for an amateur that's really good. I'm not being braggadocios either (AKA, bragging about it). I have statistics to back it up. Most of the statistics I found online say that I'm a better golfer than 96% of all golfers who keep an official handicap. Since most golfers don't actually have an official handicap, the stats say I'm better than over 99% of men who regularly golf. That's pretty good. That means that when golfing with friends, or even a random stranger I get paired with at my local course, I usually win.

But guess what, that skill cannot stand on its own. It's not even close. What I mean is, my skill as a golfer cannot stand alone as a skill that could provide value to myself or my family. Let me put it this way, if I tried to become a professional golfer, we would be homeless, starving and cold shivering under a bridge somewhere. I'm a really good golfer, but I am not even remotely skilled enough at golf to be on the PGA Tour or make a living by tournament winnings. Even if I quit my job, practiced every day, and received top-level coaching it's still out of the question.

SKILLS CAN BE LAYERED

Don't overestimate your skill. However, a skill that is above average such as my golfing ability, could be paired with another above average skill, such as teaching or having a business background, and then you could open a golf training center.

Skills can be layered.

This is a critical part in the skill identification process where we not only identify our skills but also identify how they could layer on top of each other.

> Entrepreneurial spirit + creative eye + amateur sewing skills + marketing tool (social media) = Girls Boutique Online Dress Shop

Our skills and abilities should be reviewed in order to determine how they can be layered on top of each other to create something unique. For instance, a good bun by itself doesn't make me all that hungry. A hamburger patty sitting by itself isn't very appetizing unless you're living your life carb-free which I emphatically do not. However, as you begin to layer ingredients on top of ingredients you begin to create something that people would pay to eat. So now, you take that same bun, that same hamburger patty, add some cheese, bacon, crispy onion straws, lettuce, tomato, and spicy barbecue sauce and you have something delicious. In the same exact way, as you layer skills on top of skills, talents on top of talents, you begin to create something unique and valuable. As you recognize certain skills and abilities you have which would pair nicely with others, then you can create something with exponential value to the world.

> "That means there is something inside of you which has never been seen, and will never be seen unless you grow it, cultivate and produce it for the world to consume."

Part of the layering process should be the consideration of the things we are good at but not great. Don't ignore being good at something because you've deemed it to be common. What is important to understand is that as we layer skills something great can culminate from a being good at a bunch of different things. For instance, I'm good at relating to people socially but not great. I'm a good public speaker but not world class, yet. I'm good at understanding and relaying what I've learned to others. I'm good at business. I can layer something I'm great at with a bunch of things I'm good at to create something unique. My wife wasn't a great seamstress, but she was good enough to create something simple.

The important takeaway is that there is no exact magic formula for you, except to start a list.

Listing out our skills is such an important step. Writing down our skills and talents down gives us a visualization of our abilities, an itemized list of what we do well. I can't encourage you enough to take some time and put pen to paper.

There is a page at the end of this chapter to serve as a template for this step. When you take a few minutes and begin writing down your different skills and abilities it's amazing how differently you will see yourself and your potential. You won't feel so limited or trapped anymore. You will begin to feel encouraged and inspired by a new self-realization of what your future could hold.

I meant what I said a few paragraphs ago, exponential value is somewhere hidden on the inside of each on of us. That is a very strong statement which I stand behind completely. Why? Because no two human beings on earth are exactly the same. There are about 7 billion of us on this planet and no two are identical in regard to skills, talents, abilities, aptitudes or giftings. That means there is something inside of you which has never been seen, and will never be seen unless you grow it, cultivate and produce it for the world to consume. The question isn't <u>if it can</u> happen, the question is <u>if you will make it</u> happen. When you have the mindset to start unearthing, to start digging inside of yourself and bringing concrete thoughts and ideas to the surface then the "if" of the equation has been answered and it's only a matter of "when". I hope you believe that about yourself. I hope you believe that you were put on this Earth on purpose and for a purpose. I hope you are inspired to self-evaluate and self-assess. I hope you take this first step towards discovering your own uniqueness.

You've probably heard the saying, "the sky is the limit." Well, in Isaiah 55:9, God tells us, "As the heavens are higher than the earth, so are my ways higher than your ways and my thoughts than your thoughts." Another verse I love is found in Ephesians 3:20. The verse says, "Now to Him (God) who is able to do exceedingly, abundantly above all you

> "I hope you believe that you were put on this Earth on purpose and for a purpose."

could ask or imagine." Here is what these two verses tell me: First, God's thoughts are on a different level than ours and His ways are on a different plane. Second, He is able to do more than we could ever ask for or dream about in our lives. So, it leads me to this question, if there is a God who thinks this way about me and has the ability to make the amazing happen, why should I be so attached to my plans? At some point I have to trust in both his intention and ability and allow Him to have control of my future. But here's the awesome thing, the foundation for the incredible plan for you has already been laid. God has given you skills and abilities. Those are the building blocks that God wants to use to introduce you to a life you've never even dreamed you could live.

So, I believe, for myself and for you, that the sky isn't actually the limit at all. My limit is higher than the sky when maximizing my skills. My potential is farther than the moon when I use and grow my abilities. My limit is the highest heavens and my potential is the farthest galaxies. And so is yours.

The next page is a helpful worksheet that should stay with you as you read the rest of this book. There are some instructions which will guide you on which sections to complete after reading certain chapters. It might take a few minutes, or an hour, but invest the time into yourself and your future by identifying your skills, talents, and abilities.

INSTRUCTIONS

Take time to complete the areas below after reading the following chapters. You should fill in your "Identified Skills" now. Complete your "Identified Passions" after reading Chapter 3 and "Identified Intersections" after reading Chapter 5.

Identified Skills

1.
2.
3.
4.

Identified Passions

1.
2.
3.
4.

Identified Intersections

1.   Value Assessment:
2.   Value Assessment:
3.   Value Assessment:
4.   Value Assessment:

CHAPTER 3 – WHAT ARE YOUR PASSIONS?

There is an amusement park near my hometown called Kennywood. Imagine Cedar Point or Six Flags on a smaller scale. When I was growing up, every year in late spring, our school district would have Kennywood Picnic Day. It was just about the best day of the year besides Christmas. No school and we went to ride rollercoasters all day! What could be better than that? There was a lot of planning that went into Kennywood Day. I don't mean with my parents either. There was a lot of planning that I had to do. First, was planning what would be my Kennywood Picnic Day outfit. I couldn't be looking like a bum on Kennywood Day! Next was planning which of my friends I was going to walk around with at the park. I had to make sure we would have fun but not get in trouble. (I was always the kid with a conscious thinking about the consequences if we got caught doing something we weren't supposed to be doing.) Lastly, and most importantly, was seeing how tall I was to know what rides I could ride. Like any other kid growing up I was always measuring myself against the wall in the kitchen and hoping to be tall enough to ride the best rollercoasters at Kennywood.

There was one ride in particular I was really looking forward to ride, the Laser Loop. In retrospect, the ride wasn't all that great, but to a 9-year-old it seemed amazing. However, as with most thrill rides, the best rides always have the tallest height requirement. I was always a bit shorter than the other kids in my class so riding the Laser Loop became almost a rite of passage for me. I would always stare at the cars, with all the screaming people, going around-and-around, up and down. Because of all these factors when I was about nine years old it was my dream to one day work the Laser Loop. What could be better than pushing a button and sending dozens of people on a sixty second thrill ride? I distinctly remember in grade school we were asked to draw a picture of what we wanted to do when we grew up. The other kids were busy drawing firefighters, astronauts, doctors, ballerinas, baseball players, and teachers. Not me. I knew exactly what I was going to draw. It was a picture of me standing next to a green button that said "Go!" with the epic Laser Loop gloriously depicted in the background.

I'm sure my parents were a bit concerned when they saw my finished assignment. I wonder if they got some weird looks from the other parents. "Mr. Benedetti, you must be proud of your son aspiring to a career in amusement ride operations. You seem to have a real go-getter."

THE SECOND QUESTION

Obviously, I grew out of this dream much to my parent's relief. However, the story illustrates an important distinction we all have to make: our dreams vs. our passions. A dream is not a passion and a passion is not always a dream. Our passions and our dreams are distinctly different. In the beginning of the previous chapter I talked about being realistic with our future by filtering our dreams through the lens of our skills. This chapter does not contradict the previous chapter. It actually focuses what we just learned about ourselves.

The second question is:

What am I passionate about?

What do I love doing? What would I do for free or even pay to do?

This question determines the things which we do with all our hearts. This question will help us determine the things we can and will do with excellence without being asked. Passions are not childhood dreams. We have to make that important distinction to isolate our passions worth pursuing and filter out unrealistic dreams.

If you talk to children about what they want to be when they grow up the answers are usually on the extreme ends of the spectrum, with my 9-year-old dreams being on the low end of the spectrum. For example, a response could be associated with a very rare, elite skill that the vast majority of people don't possess. Professional athletes, world-class musicians, vocalists, dancers, artists, would fall into this category. The other end of the spectrum would be responses associated with things that very easily attainable by most everyone. Often these responses are inspired by a relationship and not a true passion for the job or task itself. Kids love their 1st grade teacher and then grow up wanting to be a teacher. That's great. Being a teacher is a wonderful career; my wife was a teacher. But the important distinction is do you love teaching, or did you love a teacher? Do you have a passion for the function or is your passion more tied to a relationship or a positive experience?

PASSIONS VS. DREAMS

We have to ask ourselves these questions. We must keep digging within ourselves so we can arrive at the root passions which are inside of all of us.

Let me compare dreams and passions to show how they differ:

>Dream: Being a professional golfer
>Passion: The sport of golf

>Dream: Operating the Laser Loop
>Passion: Ensuring people have fun

>Dream: Being a 2nd grade teacher
>Passion: Teaching and seeing other people learn something new

Passions are much broader than dreams. Dreams are limiting and will narrow your vision and thus narrow your chance of a successful result. On the other hand, passions will incorporate a much larger lists of possibilities and will widen your chance of success. Do you see that in the list above? Where a dream will provide 1 or 2 job opportunities or career paths, passions will open up possibilities within entire industries. It almost goes without saying, if you (or your child) is 6'11", 250 lbs. of

"Passions are much broader than dreams."

solid muscle, can run like a deer, and knock down 25-foot jump shots all day long, then go for the NBA! If you don't have those characteristics, then being an NBA power forward probably isn't going to happen. Instead, layer your passion for basketball on top of the skill set you do have so that now the entire basketball industry can be incorporated into your future. Maybe the thing you would be most successful at is coaching basketball instead of playing basketball. Maybe you could use connections and local resources to start a summer clinic for kids. See how the possibilities open themselves up when you widen from a specific dream to a broad passion? Dreams narrow and passions widen. Don't narrow your future instead broaden it by identifying your passions instead of your dreams.

WHERE IS YOUR PASSION?

Passions are important because a passion is the fuel added to the engine of our skills that make us go farther, faster. Our skills will build a vehicle to transport us to a successful place and our passion is the fuel that propels us towards that successful destination. It is very important that we have passion for what we do if we want to have satisfaction and success. When you have an internal passion for something it makes the late nights seem a lot earlier. Passion makes the hard work something we look forward to doing. Passion gives our production purpose. We can't be living in our full potential apart from passion. Passion is required for living in our uniqueness.

I think many people are hard working. Many people achieve success in their careers. However, how many people do you know that you would describe as being passionate about their job or career? Probably not too many. I'm not talking about people great at their jobs or that even enjoy the company where they work. I am talking about people who are truly passionate about what they are doing, people who are clearly doing exactly what they were created to do. It's sad that as I think about the contacts in my phone, only a handful of people stick out to me as people who are clearly living in a place of passion.

I would say that the majority of us try to find purpose and passion OUTSIDE of our place of production. Meaning, we find purpose and passion in our family life, not work life. We find purpose and passion with our faith, not our function at the office. We find purpose and passion with hobbies not our career. Part of this entire process for me (the process of determining my own personal uniqueness) was about identifying that my frustration wasn't with my boss, my job, my career, or profession. The process was a realization that my potential wasn't being fully realized. I was trying to fulfill my purpose outside of my job. I was trying to be unique in everything but my job.

Why not all the above? I don't think it's selfish to ask that question. I don't think it's unreasonable to want to have passion surround me. I'm passionate about my wife. I'm passionate about my children. I'm passionate about my faith. But I have to check passion at the door on Monday mornings? I reject that idea. I'm choosing both passion and purpose. Because here's what I've found, purpose and passion are siblings. Passion and purpose are related. You can't fulfill your purpose without being passionate. If you are doing something passionately, then it's probably tied to your purpose and potential. So, be passionate about something.

> "Passions are important because a passion is the fuel added to the engine of our skills that make us go farther, faster. Our skills will build a vehicle to transport us to a successful place and our passion is the fuel that propels us towards that successful destination."

Maybe you are one of the lucky ones who is passionate about what you are currently doing. Awesome, stick with it and don't give up. If not, then start to assess your passions. Make a list. Make it clear. At the end of this chapter you will have a chance to clarify your passions by adding them to the list of your skills from the last chapter.

MONEY IS NOT THE SOLUTION

A word of warning when considering your passions, be careful not to include passions for jobs, careers, or businesses based on money or other people's success in a specific area. These are dangerous pitfalls that will prevent you from identifying your true and honest passions. I'll discuss the "money" aspect first.

Money or wealth does not drive your TRUE passions. Stamp it, take it to the bank. I promise you with 100% certainty that inside you is a true passion which is not solely intent on merely making more money. However, money will unquestionably try its absolute best to influence your passions. It's like money will dress up in a costume and try to disguise itself as your passion. There is a famous misquoted Bible verse, "For money is the root of all evil." Have you ever heard that quoted or said? Well, if you have then you have been told a lie. That is not a real verse. I repeat, it's incorrect. The verse actually says in 1 Timothy 6:10, "For the LOVE of money is the root of all evil." There is an enormous difference between those two statements.

There is an enormous difference between money being inherently evil and the obsession, or love of money, being an evil motivation. If money itself were evil then the Bible would be telling us to avoid the physical items which represent money or wealth (coins, bills, gold, stocks, etc.) because those physical items would be inherently evil or the possession of those items would bring evil into our lives. But that is not what the Bible says at all. The Bible says that the love, constant pursuit or obsession with money is evil.

> "Money or wealth does not drive your TRUE passions."

Don't passionately pursue money, instead passionately pursue your passions and the rest will take care of itself. I once heard someone say, "Don't seek money, seek value because money always follows value." Let me rephrase that quote, don't approach your boss and ask for more money. Instead, approach your boss and ask how you can create more value to your organization through your position. Why? Because as you increase your value then your increased value will attract the increase in finances you were originally seeking.

SEEK VALUE

We have to be sure to detach our heart from pursuing money. Instead, we should be pursuing our passions and pursuing ways to increase our value. We ought to be value seekers. We ought to be thinking about how we can find value, create value, improve value, and bring value. This goes far beyond just our current jobs or with our current employers. This concept is what is in operation in our national economy, in all local business, and even in the global economy. Increase follows value. Increase your value and you increase you.

Money and finances are terrible navigators for one's life. The pursuit of money will cloud your mind and make it difficult to properly see your true passions. As you consider the question of "What am I passionate about?", eliminate all considerations that are founded in the easiest path to wealth. Why? For two main reasons. One, because motivations rooted in a pursuit of money alone does not have enough long-term fuel to sustain your purpose. Two, because motivations rooted in a pursuit of money will lead you away from value creation.

Greed is fleeting but passion is lasting. Money is temporary but value is permanent. Things that are truly valuable stand the test of time. Musicians that learn how to consistently produce value have sustained careers and don't become one-hit-wonders. Businesses which decide to be constantly providing more value to customers don't go out of business. Adding value to a product could be done through lowering the price. Increasing value could be an improvement to make a product or experience better. Adding value is valuable regardless of the product or industry.

I have three young children, so Disney World is a relevant vacation destination for our family right now. Walt Disney himself created, and the current leadership team have maintained, a world class culture that is continually and constantly increasing their value. Their corporate culture is consistently considering, "How can our current product be more valuable to our consumers? What can we do different or new that would be of value to our consumers?" Sometimes increasing value to customers is tearing down an older attraction in Disney World so they can construct something new which will create demand for tickets. They hold onto the iconic, brand defining rides and structures, but the rest is all subject to change. Disney isn't in the game for the short-term results, but they are steadfast in long-term value creation. As a result, their commitment to value drives their decisions.

> "We ought to be value seekers. We ought to be thinking about how we can find value, create value, improve value, and bring value."

So how can a person tell if their passion is value motivated or money motivated? Depth. Passions carry a depth which cannot be satisfied by material possessions or superficial changes. Your passions should be deeper than a longing for a nice car or house. These are both fine things and to some extent necessities in our modern world. There has to be something deeper than ourselves or material possessions driving our motives towards change. Depth was how I knew the feelings inside of me weren't just the desires of wanting something new. Depth was how I knew the motivations inside of me were pushing me towards purpose. Depth was how I knew it was a true passion. I believe the passions which are inside of you were put there so you can fulfill your

God given purpose on Earth. As you pursue your passions, I'm confident that you can create something valuable and see your family blessed beyond your wildest expectations.

COMPARISON KILLS

The second trap to discuss is allowing someone else's success to influence, or even dictate, your passions. It's great to have friends, relatives, neighbors, or co-workers who are successful and serve as inspiration to our lives. However, it can be very easy to walk into a trap whereby we are trying to imitate or replicate someone's success that came as a result of someone else's passion.

I have a great friend who is an awesome salesman. He has worked on his technique, read countless books, and as a result, become a very success salesman at a large multi-national corporation. He tells me that from time-to-time he is approached by someone much younger asking what he or she might need to do to in order to have similar success in sales. They come to him hoping to learn about a trick or trade secret that will effortlessly send them straight to the top. My friend then begins to layout an overview of all the hard work they will need to invest in order to see the same results he has experienced. He recommends that they read specific books and work certain hours. He tells them that he can mentor them, but they will be strictly held accountable to the high standards he sets. He asks them to produce results and typically, over time, most of his proteges lose focus and stop their ascent.

> "Passions carry a depth which cannot be satisfied by material possessions or superficial changes."

What happened? Were they less skilled? Not necessarily. Were they less talented? Not necessarily. They lacked the passionate pursuit that my friend had developed for sales and leadership. His passion was for the process. Most of the other men and women he mentored had only had passion for the paycheck or end result product.

Passion should always be tied to a process and not a product. Because the value created from a process will outlast and outgrow the value created by chasing a product or end result. If you try to emulate or replicate someone else, then you will inevitably end up being a cheap copy. Now, I'm not very knowledgeable about art sales or the value of pieces of art. But I do know that originals are much more expensive than copies. In some cases, the originals are infinitely more expensive than their replications. The point is that the world can always detect a fake. My wife can spot a fake Louis Vuitton handbag across a crowded room and our culture usually doesn't take too long to identify when we are a cheap replica of someone else. On the other hand, when the market finds something truly original, well look out. When something original is found in the fashion, food, or entertainment industries then enormous value is created.

Each person reading these words has a true and honest passion on the inside. Your true passions could be traced all the way back to your childhood, or maybe it's a brand-new discovery. Regardless of when they started, they are there, and they are there for a reason. Don't ignore them any longer. Maybe you have a passion to entertain or make people happy. It's not a dream of operating a rollercoaster, it's a passion to bring joy to others. Don't ignore that. Whether your passion is tied to our local Main Street or Wall Street, whether it's for business or arts, whether it's for teaching or creating, don't ignore them. Discover your passions, then embrace and incubate them.

Go ahead and take out the same piece of paper that has the list of your skills from the last chapter and complete the section for Chapter 3 by listing out your true passions. Begin writing down your passions. Forget about your childhood dreams. Forget about those dreams that narrow and limit possibilities. Don't list your parents or your co-worker's passions. Don't write what you wish you were passionate about but write down the passions in your heart. It doesn't matter how seemingly insignificant they might be in your mind; they might be the starting point of something amazing. Walt Disney built an empire around one mouse. One little cartoon mouse named Mickey birthed a multi-billion-dollar organization. One man was passionate about his mouse and refused to stop dreaming of where that mouse could take him. Isn't that encouraging to hear? It inspires me to dream about where my passions could take me.

Allow yourself a few minutes to think through and make a list. I would advise to not continue until you feel you have a generated a thorough list of both your passions and skills. As we move onto the following chapters, this list will be vitally important in helping you determine your uniqueness. After identifying our skills and passions we must take the next step. The next chapter will help you to take that next step.

41

CHAPTER 4 – WHERE DO YOUR SKILLS INTERSECT WITH YOUR PASSIONS?

Have you ever gotten into your car and started driving somewhere only to realize you drove to the wrong place? I can remember a few months ago needing to run an errand and my mind was wondering while I was driving. Maybe I was thinking about what I needed to get done that day. Maybe I was thinking about a work project or listening to a really interesting podcast. Regardless of the distraction, before I knew it, I drove in completely the wrong direction for 10 minutes. I can remember driving to work on a Sunday morning instead of driving to church. I was wearing the same clothes I wear to work. I was in the car about the same time in the morning. It is almost like my instincts overrode my brain. I can recall thinking "where am I going?"

Maybe you've never had that particular situation happen, but I'd bet if you are over 28 years old you can remember a time driving without a smartphone or GPS unit. I can remember getting directions off friends, "You'll see an old gas station named 'Billy's Gas' turn left and then go about a mile and make a right when you see a tree shaped like a wizard's walking stick." I can also remember printing off maps from MapQuest. Those maps were awesome as long as you stayed on the highlighted route. I can remember driving being completely lost. Am I on the right road? How long do I drive until I should stop and ask? Whenever I got lost, I always did the dumbest thing, I would drive faster. My thought process was the faster I drove, the quicker I will know if I'm off my desired route. What did happen though is I would just end up even more lost, if that's even a thing. Maybe it's a guy thing, I'm not sure. One thing I do know, the invention of GPS is proof there is a God in heaven. God loved us so much he sent GPS into our lives to save us, and our marriages.

Where am I going? Am I on the right path? I have had those same thoughts related to my career before as well. Where am I going with my career? Am I even headed down the right path? Those two questions are what this chapter will address, where should we be going and how do we know if we are on the right path.

In keeping with the vehicle theme, this chapter is where the rubber meets the road, so to speak. This chapter will take our thoughtful lists from the previous two chapters and help guide and steer us in a direction towards our purpose. Our skills are like the vehicles to take us somewhere new. Our passions are the fuel that gives our skills movement, longevity, and power. But where are we going? What address do we key into the destination field in the GPS unit of our lives?

THE THIRD QUESTION

In order to determine the destination, we must ask ourselves this third question:

Where do my skills intersect with my passions?

The intersection of our skills and our passions is the epicenter of your own uniqueness. Where do my skills and my passions overlap and connect? I talked about layering skills in chapter 3. This idea isn't as much about combining skills with passions but identifying what skills and passions are <u>complementary</u> of one another. Skills and passions can complement one another or conflict with one another.

My wife is awesome in the kitchen. She is especially a wonderful baker. Whenever we are invited to our friends' houses, she is almost always asked to bring a dessert. In my humble, but well-educated, opinion pies are her particular specialty. She makes an incredible apple, blueberry, pumpkin, and my personal favorite, coconut cream. The secret is in her crust. It's actually my favorite part. She has found the different ingredients which complement one another and thus enhance the taste of what she is creating. This even goes for her crust. The flakey, sweet crust she makes isn't just to house the pie filling, but it enhances the overall taste of the pie. The same concept is perfectly applicable with the consideration of our skills and passions. Our skills need to complement our passions. When combined in the right way our skills and passions actually complement one another and create something valuable.

What skills do you have that when done passionately would be exciting to you and valuable to someone else? Maybe you have a skill for social media marketing and a passion for disabled children. That skill of social media marketing could be used to help non-profits better promote and inform of their organizations to help children, fundraise for donations, or recruit new employees. Maybe you have a skill for business law and a passion to help young entrepreneurs. That particular legal skill and expertise could be used in many ways to help advise and guide entrepreneurs to avoid pitfalls during the creation of their new business entities. Seek to identify your passions that complement your skills. Seek to identify your skills that pair with a passion and create something valuable.

> "What skills do you have that when done passionately would be exciting to you and valuable to someone else?"

By identifying skills and passions, and then isolating the potential value that could be created by overlapping the two, you have added a '/' unique to your own skill set. Think of it this way, if our skills always ran parallel to our passions then the two forces would never encounter each other to create a new experience. At some point our skills must intersect with our passions in order to combine together and create something truly unique and valuable. This is the most critical part of the process because this is where we determine our uniqueness. Uniqueness is a mixture of part skill and part passion. Here's the exciting part, the greater amount of your various skills you can intersect with your strongest passions will end up creating the largest possible intersections. Think about Chip Gaines for this point.

SEIZING THE OPPORTUNITY

You know who Chip Gaines is, right? The husband of Joanna Gaines. One of the co-stars on *Fixer Upper* on HGTV. I listened to his audio book 'Capital Gaines' recently and noticed something about his "brand". Chip was a self-described entrepreneur. He started and ran many businesses before most of us ever heard about him. He started in landscaping, then moved into rental properties. Next, he started flipping houses and got his real estate license. Also, during this time, he and Joanna opened a successful retail store, Magnolia Market. After all of that he began remodeling and doing construction. He had his hands in a bunch of different pots. But if you've ever watched his show you can easily tell that his personality is perfect for TV. Not acting, but being on the exact kind of show which made him wildly famous, reality TV. He is funny and witty. He is goofy and balances his wife's more straight-forward, calm personality. His uniqueness was already discovered and in operation long before he filmed his first episode of *Fixer Upper*. But he wasn't able to fully utilize his skill of humor and passion for entertaining until the opportunity was presented. So, notice how the two parts of his very successful puzzle came to fit perfectly together:

First, when the opportunity came along to enter into a new career of reality TV Chip didn't then have to develop an engaging and outgoing personality. He didn't have to start working on how to be entertaining or develop a personality that would cause others to binge watch him do demolition. He was already ready for that component. There is a part we play in our own preparation to ensure that our uniqueness is ready when needed. This isn't to say that Chip didn't improve as the TV series was renewed year-after-year. This isn't to say that Chip was a finished product on day one of filming. However, it is to say that the foundation needed for him to be successful was already laid. The rest was improvements and tweaks.

> "This taught me a valuable lesson, time in preparation is not wasted time."

This taught me a valuable lesson, time in preparation is not wasted time. The time spent in preparation is so vital in determining what our future holds and raising our ceiling of potential. In Chip's life you can see that before he ever began doing remodeling in front of cameras, he had honed his skills with no cameras. Chip was able to demonstrate repeated excellence with no audience before there was ever a national TV audience.

Second, when the TV cameras and national TV show increased his outlet for his uniqueness, he increased his value. He didn't just increase his value a little, he was able to increase is value a lot. As his new outlet (television) drew on his unique skill sets and passions he experienced personal and financial growth at a rapid pace. Think of it this way, the size (or volume) of the outflow of your uniqueness is directly correlated to the growth of your value. It's the principle of supply and demand. Too much demand is an awesome problem to have. In fact, it's a much better problem than too little demand. It means people want what you are selling. They want to buy your goods and they want to use your services. But an abundance of demand can create issues to work through.

The first, and biggest one, is can you meet the demands being placed upon you? That is where supply comes into the picture. If you have a large supply waiting in advance of a big demand, then you are in perfect place to see huge growth. That's the way I see it with Chip Gaines. He had built up a store house, a huge supply of uniqueness. He had skills by the boxful. He had passion oozing from his pores. He has a big store of personality and a world class work ethic. All of this meant a lot of uniqueness in supply. Then, and because of his regional success, a national demand came as opportunity dressed up as TV cameras. The intense demand was able to be fully met, and then some, because of the great supply of uniqueness.

PREPARTION IS PROGRESS

It's almost as if all those years of working in relative anonymity weren't wasted at all. In fact, it seems to me that those years were valuable in the maturation process to develop Chip and Joanna into becoming a TV and marketing powerhouse. He was ready when his uniqueness met opportunity. Joanna was ready as a designer when her unique style and eye met opportunity. Then, as the TV show gained popularity, they were able to remain grounded in their true unique identity and kept doing what they always did, create value. This time their value creation wasn't limited to small store fronts and rental properties. Now they are creating value with books, entire sections at Target, restaurants, businesses, large retail outlets, and who knows what else they have in their hearts to accomplish.

What good is it to have opportunity but nothing to offer? Conversely, what good is it to have something to offer but no opportunity? Enough with Chip and Joanna, this is the way I see it in my own life. What I offer is up to me, the opportunity part is up to God. Meaning this, I am responsible for developing and working on myself. I am responsible to getting off my butt, asking hard questions of myself, isolating what needs improved, and then doing what needs done to see change happen. I am responsible for doing my part to see myself improve and develop. Here's why, if you're not skilled at what you are doing, then what you're doing will be common and ordinary. If you're not passionate about your work, then it will get old and lack excellence. That's why it's our responsibility to develop our skills, to nurture our passions and then find where they intersect and collide. We can't just expect to offer common and ordinary to the world and expect the customers to come in droves. But let me tell you, if you can do something you love, and something you're awesome at, it won't be common or ordinary. It will be unique and special. People will drive to see something unique. People will pay to purchase something special.

My brother-in-law is another example of the principle of developing yourself in preparation for something on the horizon. My youngest sister's husband, let's call him Mike, graduated college with a degree in youth ministry. He took a position at a church in Ohio as one of their youth pastors. Over several years of diligently working and serving those kids, he honed and developed his ability to connect with other people. He studied how to develop communities within communities to better connect people into positive relationships. Eventually his skills led him farther down this particular path of ministry and his passions were more concentrated in this area as well. As a result, he was offered a position at a church in a nearby town. But wait, it gets better. My brother-in-law, Mike, is a serious sport enthusiast. He grew up in the Cleveland suburbs and, unfortunately for him, loves all Cleveland sports. Yes, even the Browns! I would definitely say that sports are a passion of his.

> "I am responsible to getting off my butt, asking hard questions of myself, isolating what needs improved, and then doing what needs done to see change happen. I am responsible for doing my part to see myself improve and develop."

After a few years at his new position, through various connections, he was offered the position of team chaplain for one of Cleveland's professional sports franchises. What if he would have stopped developing his abilities to connect? What if he just assumed that he would always be a youth pastor? Then, he would have been unqualified and out of position to do something truly unique and rare.

You have been uniquely created to be passionately doing something you are skilled to do. Let me restate that last sentence more emphatically, YOU (not your neighbor, friend or co-worker) have been uniquely created (there is no one just like you in the entire Earth) to be passionately (with all your heart) doing something you are skilled (expertly gifted) to do.

So, take out the lists I know you created based on the previous two chapters. Aren't you glad you made a list of both your skills and passions? If they are on separate pieces of paper put them side-by-side or even considering merging them into one document or using the page provided at the end of Chapter 1. Now look at them. Review them. Tweak and add to them. Stare at them some more. Write them down and get them in front of your eyes. Study them again. It might seem weird or awkward to do but spend a few minutes just allowing those details to resonate into your mind.

Human beings are so very creative. We are the only species on Earth that has the cognitive ability to think critically and then create and build. All other species are limited to creating only out of necessity, like nests or simple homes. I've never seen a monkey make a simple wheel or bicycle let alone a computer motherboard, electric vehicles or a 110-story skyscraper. Our brains are engineered to create. So how do we activate the creative nature within us? By putting something on paper in front of our eyes to see. When we present our eyes with the ingredients of our skills and passions, we've identified that are most valuable inside of us, it's like giving bags of groceries to a master chef.

> "You have been uniquely created to be passionately doing something you are skilled to do."

When I did this simple exercise of writing down my skills and passions it made the process of determining my uniqueness so much clearer since I could see intersections being formed and created. It wasn't like a tiny bell went off or a small light bulb came on as I reviewed my lists, it was like sirens were blaring and police lights flashing on a dark night. I remember asking myself, "How could I have lived so long with this potential inside of me going undiscovered?" The answer? The trap. It was the Potential Trap keeping me from traveling where I was in the safety of my profession towards the intersection of my uniqueness.

The Bible tells us in Proverbs 18:16, "that our gifts will bring us before great men." Do you believe that? I truly believe that, for not only myself but for you as well. When we discover what is unique about us, we truly discover the thing that we were destined and born to do. Our gifts and skills, when done passionately, create our uniqueness which will place us into an atmosphere of greatness and influence. Why? Because each human God has ever created is valuable and contains the ability to tap into their full, God-purposed potential.

It is crucial to fully believe that our gifts will bring us before great men. This belief goes hand-in-hand with the process of discovering your own personal uniqueness. You can't have one without the other. I'm not sure which comes first, but it is necessary and crucial to have a vision larger than your current situation and then work to discover and live out your unique you. The mindset is the driving motivation behind fine tuning and persevering into your unique intersection when roadblocks and potholes present themselves.

The next chapter will help you to identify where your own unique intersections might be hiding in plain sight. It will also help you to determine how, and when, they might fit in your future.

SECTION 2 – DETERMINING THE PATH TO TAKE

CHAPTER 5 – FINDING A FIT FOR YOUR UNIQUENESS

F it is an important consideration when making a decision. Actually, let me phrase that more accurately, fit can make or break you. This point is made crystal clear through fashion. And few fashion decisions are quite as important as the fashion choices made during the ever-so formative high school years (that was typed with extreme sarcasm, by the way). When I was in my early high school years, I started to become more interested in clothes and fashion. I don't mean that I was becoming more interested in designing them or pursuing the fashion industry, but I was becoming more and more aware of what I was wearing to school to make sure I was one of the "cool" kids. I can feel your eyes rolling right now. Don't worry, so are mine. I was constantly asking myself, "Does this match? Is this the right style? What will people think about my outfit? It is cool or lame? Should I wear this shirt tucked, untucked or ever-so the trendy front-tuck?" You know, questions that a lot of insecure high school kids ask themselves. Well anyways, what I can tell you is that fourteen-year-old Mark was much more concerned about the look of the style rather than the fit of the actual clothes being worn. I was always small for my age, but I wouldn't let my slight frame stop me from buying what I thought were cool clothes. In fact, I was so eager to wear stonewashed carpenter jeans from American Eagle Outfitters that I can remember buying a pair of these magnificent pants that were easily two inches too big in the waistline. Now this was the mid-90's but I didn't purchase them big on purpose. I bought the smallest waistline they offered and decided I was going to force them to work. All I cared about was the style and didn't think for a second about the fit. I thought, "I have a belt. I'll just pull on the belt until they are just tight enough to not fall down to my ankles." I look back at pictures during those years and ask my mom why she didn't intervene a bit more with some motherly guidance like, "You look silly. Get in the car right now, we are returning those parachute pants."

As an adult I now understand that fit is critical. Proper fit is crucial to our clothes if our intention is for them to complement our physical appearance. Style and design are not enough anymore. Style and design must align with fit for our clothes to look the best. Everyone is different and everyone's body is different. I'm sure, no matter your size that finding something that fits just right is half the battle. In the same way, proper fit is absolutely necessary for our identified unique intersection if we desire our pursuits to succeed. We have to find something that fits. This isn't always the easiest thing and you can't force it to fit, even fourteen-year-old Mark knows this.

> "Finding fit matters. Finding perfect fit is crucial."

Sometimes we might discover something unique about us but aren't sure how to fit it into our lives or the world around us. Sometimes we must put things back on the shelf, not because we are giving up, but because it doesn't fit just right, for just right now. Finding fit matters. Finding perfect fit is crucial.

FINDING WHAT FITS

That's what this chapter is all about. Helping you answer the question, "How do I determine if the intersections of my uniqueness I've just identified are a good fit?" Hopefully you have taken the time to invest in yourself by taking inventory of your skills and passions. At the end of this chapter, you will be prompted to identify intersections worth pursuing.

Here are some questions you might be asking, "How do I know if the intersections I've identified are worth pursuing? If I have identified multiple intersections, which ones should I start moving towards?" All these questions are great to ask and need consideration and diligent thought. The quick answer lies within each intersection's potential value. Identifying the potential value that your intersections could provide will determine the priority of your efforts. Meaning, how much value can possibly be created by my efforts in building something at the intersection of my identified skills and passions?

Value creation should be the main driver behind our decisions to move towards an intersection and build something there. Please consider, value does not mean only profitability. Value is much broader and can represent different things to different people. Value is defined as "something considered to be important, beneficial or having worth." Value is actually a prerequisite for profitability. Meaning there must be value before there can financial profit.

Value always precedes profit. Value always exists before we trade our finances for something we have deemed valuable. Let me prove it to you. When you go to Wal-Mart you see something on a shelf, you see the price to buy the item and then you trade your money for that item. The product exists before you hand over your hard-earned money, right? You might be thinking right now of other scenarios that could disprove my theory. Well, what about a charitable contribution? We don't receive a good or service from that transaction. Maybe we don't receive a good or service but there is value created before our finances are sent. We value the mission, the purpose of the charity or we value helping someone in need. We possibly even value the internal feeling that comes from contributing and being a part of our beloved charities. Value always precedes finances. Like I said in Chapter 3, seek value and finances will follow. Increase your value or create something valuable and money will surely follow.

> "Value creation should be the main driver behind our decisions to move towards an intersection and build something there."

You have identified your uniqueness and isolated which intersections are valuable, or have the most value potential, now where or how do we fit our valuable uniqueness into our lives and world? One way to help isolate where value can be created is to identify where a need exists. Where is there a need which my uniqueness can help resolve? Where is there a problem that my uniqueness, my intersection answers? Is there a need in my community? Is there a need to the greater population that I can fulfill using the internet or technology?

VALUE DETERMINES FIT

Proper fit occurs when we match our valuable uniqueness with an existing need. Like matching an outfit, we also must match our intersection to a need we can fulfill. So, if you've determined you are uniquely good at baking or cooking the next step is to determine how you deliver your food to the right people in the market. Do you open a restaurant or bakery? Do you sell from your home kitchen? Do you utilize an online food delivery service? Fit your uniqueness into a need and you create something valuable.

This is potentially the hardest question to answer because we have to leave the stage where we are examining ourselves and now, we must examine our culture, community, and surroundings to fit our uniqueness into the right place. This may be a difficult part of the process for you, but it surely is an essential part in order to achieve success. Who wants to have a skill and God-given passion without seeing it successful? This is the part where we must do our homework.

I thought it would be helpful to your process if I walked you through my exact process of identifying my skills and passions, determining my uniqueness, and then finding a fit for my uniqueness. I'll also share some intersections I identified that I could not find a fit for, either permanently or at the present moment.

How did my idea to write a book come from that mixture of skills and passions? Back to my story, I was cutting the grass on a humid Saturday afternoon in the middle of September in southwestern Pennsylvania and these thoughts kept bouncing around my head. Asking myself, "What can I do next?" Asking God, "What have you purposed for me to do?" These questions ping-ponging around in my head weren't creating frustration and anger, they were building a longing desire to discover. Earlier that same week, I was spending time in prayer and I believe God spoke to me, no in fact I know God spoke to me, and gave me the three questions I just outlined in the earlier chapters. God asked me, "What are your skills? What are your passions? Where do your skills intersect with your passions? That intersection is where your uniqueness is found." His questions were leading me down a path of self-discovery. He told me I would find my uniqueness at that very intersection if I was willing and diligent to follow the path. So, I was cutting the grass thinking about my skills. I was emptying the wheelbarrow thinking about my passions. I was thinking about ways that I could create value by using skills fueled by my passions.

> "Who wants to have a skill and God-given passion without seeing it successful?"

As I was doing yard-work, I identified my skill set to be public speaking, developing leadership and self-improvement content, business and accounting, teaching, relating to others easily and naturally, personal financial coaching, creating energetic atmospheres, making people laugh, and thinking creatively.

As I was pulling weeds, I determined that I'm passionate about crowds (I'd much rather be in a big city than in the country), being around other people, public speaking, advising or consulting people, leadership, the local church, accounting, finding solutions to problems, and golf.

I was able to identify several intersections from these lists. By layering skills and pairing skills with passions, I was able to generate a possibilities list. Some were obvious and full of potential and some were under the surface or even odd. Here is a list of what I came up showing the linkage of my skills and passions creating various intersections:

Skills	+ Passion	= Intersection
Accounting knowledge	Consulting others	Accounting firm
Teaching others	Golf	Golf training center
Making people laugh	Big crowds	Stand-up comedian
Public speaking	Advising/consulting	Leadership consultant
Thinking creatively	Leadership	Author

EVALUATING VALUE

Even at first glance some of those intersections listed above seem more realistic and probable than others. Each one has its own set of challenges and opportunities. Let me list each one and then illustrate the thought process behind determining if the intersection should be passed over or pursued with passion.

Accounting Firm - This is a possibility with my professional credentials and work experience. I have worked in two regional accounting firms and am familiar with the industry. There is a lot of upside with this line of business as accounting firms can be very profitable. They also require a great deal of effort to stay current on all the changes within accounting standards and tax law. Although I have the skill set that would lend to bringing in new clients, researching and learning tax law is definitely not a passion of mine. Decision - Pass, unlikely in future

Golf Training Center - I love golf and I'm really good for an amateur, however, I'd need someone qualified as a teaching professional to lend credibility upon opening. This would require a significant amount of investment to purchase land, equipment, and build a facility. Regionally, there isn't something like this, however, western Pennsylvania isn't the ideal climate either. This could be a future endeavor based upon finances and if a business partner is necessary. Decision - Pass, possible in future

Stand-up Comedian - I just laughed out loud after even typing this intersection. Don't get me wrong, making people laugh is a great feeling. I don't feel as though this aligns with my family values at the moment. I've listened to comedians discuss their travel life and it is always described as extensive. Ultimately, while I enjoy this socially, I don't feel drawn to this professionally. Decision - Pass, unlikely in future

Leadership Consultant - I feel strongly about this intersection as well. My skills align with a lot of what is needed, running a business, developing content, public speaking, being engaging and inspirational. I'm passionate about helping others and delivering an encouraging message is just about one of the best feelings in the world. At the present moment, my platform needs to be developed and grown to be a driver behind generating engagements to speak or consult. Decision - Pass, very likely in future as next step

As I processed through my skills and passions it became clear that my uniqueness could be found in helping others through encouragement and guidance. So, if the intersection of my skills and passions pointed to being an advisor/speaker/consultant/author the next step was to determine how to do I find a fit for this uniqueness in the world? I know the product to offer but I still did not know the medium to disperse the product. How do I offer this service to the world and have it pay the bills? I thought of podcasts. Maybe I could start a podcast. I thought of business consulting. Maybe I could try to start a consulting firm. As I began to think through how that could happen, or if it were even feasible, the mounting frustration drove to me to action. I began to have this thought strain in my mind:

> I wonder how many other people feel like me. I wonder how many other people feel trapped by their current job. I bet there are a lot of people frustrated by these same issues, having these same thoughts. But I bet there aren't that many people who know what to do next. I ought to write down how we can be trapped at times but how adding a slash can be a solution. I ought to journal these ideas. I should journal this concept and the steps to overcome being limited by one thing and how to become many things. Maybe it would help somebody.

I immediately left my lawnmower in the yard and started typing. I started writing out all these ideas that were swirling in my head. The process was like opening a door and allowing a tornado to exit my house just by putting pen to paper (or more accurately, by putting fingers to a keyboard). For me, the process of writing felt like I opened a valve on a pressure tank which was about to explode. At first, I thought I was scripting out a message to be preached at church or possibly a leadership series for our church's quarterly leadership seminars. Before I realized it, I had been typing for over 2 hours and had about 8 pages of this book started. My wife came home from running some errands and I sat her in front of the laptop and told her to read. She finished reading the 8 pages I had written and asked me, "What is this?" I responded, "I think it's a book."

"The Potential Trap tried to silence my newfound ambition by doubt, facts and even fears."

At that moment a '/' was added and an author was born.

Funny thing though, when you find your purpose the Potential Trap will try to convince you otherwise. The trap tried to silence my newfound ambition by doubt, facts and even fears. The negative voice in my head was screaming,

"Write a book? You can't even write a postcard! Maybe if you were a pastor or a CEO, but who will read a book you write?"

I silenced the voice of negativity and kept moving towards my intersection. The more I wrote, the more fulfilled I felt. I told myself, "Yes, maybe my writing skills aren't as high as my speaking skills, however, skills can be improved upon and grown. This utilizes the same passions as leadership consulting, but just through a different medium. This utilizes the same ability to engage and encourage but just through a different method. My work could stand on its own and I wouldn't need significant capital to start."

As quickly as negativity can have a debilitating snowball effect, positivity can have a productive snowball effect just as fast. If you allow negativity to dictate your thoughts, then most likely your intersections will crumble to pieces. Be patient to the process and protect your intersection with guardrails of a positive disposition. Finding a fit for our uniqueness is a process. Sometimes it goes quickly. Sometimes it takes time. Sometimes it comes naturally. Sometimes it's like pulling teeth.

> "As quickly as negativity can have a debilitating snowball effect, positivity can have a productive snowball effect just as fast."

Once you have identified the potential value within an intersection the very next two questions that need asked and answered are these:

1. Is this a fit for now?
2. What outside resources, if any, do I need to convert this from an idea into a reality?

NOW OR LATER

As I mentioned above, you might identify an intersection that has great potential value and utilizes your skills and passions but seems like it's too far of a reach to start now. It is not negative thinking to take a realistic inventory of your current situation. Meaning, if you identified an intersection of owning and running a nationwide trucking and logistics company, if you have identified there is a need for your particular idea, and if you have identified value to your idea, THEN you must identify if this idea is one you can start now.

Can you begin your adventure now, or is this something you pin in your vision board for later? Odds are you might not have the resources (or maybe your dad is Bill Gates and you do) to purchase the assets, customer base, and whatever else would need done to move directly into this particular industry. However, you can start with where you are now. Maybe you can start with one truck and look to rapidly expand. Whatever the idea, you have to determine if the end goal is for now or later.

If I'm being honest, I'm not sure where authoring this book will take me in life. I have some hopes and dreams. I have some plans and aspirations, but what I know for certain is that writing it was the next step. Do what you can do now and don't get caught up if it takes some time to approach the finish line. Chances are the finish line will end up changing en route anyways. Bill Gates started his company trying to build computers. However, along the way he realized that developing software could be even more lucrative.

> "There might be a time in your life when you come to the realization that the fulfillment of your dream might depend on someone else..."

A HELPING HAND

The second question to consider is if your identified intersection will require outside resources to see it come to fruition. There might be a time in your life when you come to the realization that the fulfillment of your dream might depend on someone else to either help you get going or share in your dream and work alongside you. This happened to my wife and I in 2017.

In early January 2017, during a time of prayer, my wife and I came in agreement that God was instructing us to pursue opening a Peace Love and Little Donuts franchise in our area. We took this instruction and began to research and investigate this exciting business idea at a ferocious pace.

Just to give a little background to the franchise, Peace Love and Little Donuts was founded in Pittsburgh and, as of January 2019, has about 40 locations nationwide. The franchise serves coffee and, as the name states, little donuts which are a touch smaller than a slider. The donuts are all cake and are freshly made in the store all day long. Each plain donut is then topped in front of the customer with over 50 options to choose between from classic icing and sprinkles to donuts with fancy, creative toppings. My favorites flavors are Raspberry Truffle and Salted Carmel Macchiato. Yea, they are incredibly good. The entire store is 70's themed and tie-dye painted.

We happened to know, through various connections, two people who already owned franchises in other towns. We contacted them to find out the cost involved, the time involved and if their investment (in both time and money) has been worthwhile. The response we received was overwhelmingly positive. However, one consistent word of caution was that this particular investment would require hands-on involvement. To do it right and to make money, each franchise owner we sat down with said the same thing, "You will need to spend time, lots of time in the store. You can't hire people and expect them to care about your product and customers like you will. You have to be present or you will struggle having operations run smoothly." Basically, the message was, you can't be an absentee owner. This isn't a "set it and forget it" type operation. Hmm. Well this was not ideal for our situation. I had a full-time job, which often required overtime, that would prevent me from being an "on-call" donut maker. And my wife? Well, she was about 1 month pregnant with our third child. Not exactly the ideal situation for aspiring entrepreneurs looking to open a business requiring a lot of focused attention and daily management.

The moment we arrived at the conclusion that we couldn't do it alone was a critical, crucial, massive juncture. If you could envision us standing at an intersection having to decide which direction to take. Our options were the following:

A. Path 1 - Give up and ignore the idea. Forget about the instruction we received from God. Delete a '/' from being added to our self-definition.

B. Path 2 - Delay until the timing fits our situation better. Maybe we could wait until our son was one year old and then make it work by sending him to daycare.

C. Path 3 - Find business partners who could share in our vision and the effort needed to open and manage a successful franchise location.

We chose path 3. We quickly thought of our great friends from church who had previously owned a restaurant. We also knew that they were always looking for new investment ideas. We knew that the wife of the couple on our minds was looking to work daylight hours as her children were high school age.

You can look at challenges as roadblocks or speed bumps. They aren't the same. This challenge of investing the time needed to successfully operate a donut shop wasn't insurmountable. It was achievable. It was only a speed bump, not a roadblock. Our friend's situation, strengths and background were able to check off the boxes of everything my wife and I couldn't check off. They complemented us just as much as we complemented them. The partnership wasn't just a good idea, it was an ideal situation. Their hands helped ours and ours helped them.

TYPES OF HELPING HANDS

Outside resources can come in a few different forms. Here are a few:

1. **A Business Loan**

You might realize upon the research phase of your identified intersection that you don't possess the necessary resources to start your new adventure. A loan would be an option for those individuals to expedite saving to fund on your own. Now, full disclosure, I am a huge advocate against debt. In my opinion, the only permissible personal debt is a home mortgage. That means no car loans, no car leases (which are worse than car loans), quickly paying off any student loan debt, and absolutely, never-ever any credit card debt. However, debt for production is different than debt for consumption. Dave Ramsey won't agree with me on this one, however, in my opinion debt incurred that will create financial streams of income otherwise not attainable is better than years of saving and waiting. When my wife and I opened that donut franchise in 2017, we needed a small home equity loan to get started. The amount wasn't enormous and didn't bring pressure or stress into our lives. Also, starting that business has given us an additional cash flow, on top of my salary, to start other businesses by reinvesting profits. Of course, if you have the cash to fully fund a new business without a loan then you are in the best-case scenario. If not, and if your idea has potential and value, then see a small, manageable loan as a temporary means to a debt-free future. However, the determination of the need to obtain a small loan is not a decision to simply glaze over.

You need to be sure of the financial viability of your new business. Do your homework.

2. **An Investor or Investor Group**

A way to raise capital without debt is to bring investors into your idea. An investor would provide capital in exchange for ownership in your business or company. Be very careful if you identify close friends or family as potential investors. Business decisions, market pressures, and financial results (especially poor results) can put a strain on even the best family or friendships. If the strain or pressure creates a volatile situation it could quickly sever and end a relationship. These, family and close friendships, are the last relationships that should be ended and should be protected. These are people that should providing support for our unique intersection, not stress. If you do find someone able to invest in your idea, be very diligent and thorough to clearly define, in writing, the roles and responsibilities of each party. This will provide structure and a baseline of understanding as you move forward.

3. **A Partnership**

Without delving too deep into Business 101 materials, a partnership is good options for individuals who will need the resources or expertise of another person to start and/or run the operations of the new idea. When my wife and I were researching the idea of opening our donut shop we quickly came to the realization that a partnership would be needed to do this successfully. As I mentioned, we identified the areas we needed support and help. We then identified individuals who were skilled to meet those needs and people who had the ability to invest as partners. We formed a legal partnership, through a licensed attorney. As a side note, anybody unwilling to sign a formal, and legally binding, partnership document probably won't make a good partner. It has worked out to be a great partnership as each couple had access to capital to start the business and each couple brings unique skills to the enterprise. However, just as I warned when choosing an investor, use the same caution when determining with whom to form a partnership. A quality business partner will be like-minded with you. This doesn't mean they have the same skills or background. This means they have the same passion to see the venture succeed and they have the same goal for what the venture will produce.

Don't let your idea sit on the shelf collecting dust in your brain. Find a fit for it. Don't force the fit but find something that fits you. Find out of how you can fit it into the marketplace. Find out if fits for now or later. Find out if someone else will help with the fit.

Something fits you. You fit something. Find it.

CHAPTER 6 – REFINE YOURSELF

As I mentioned in the last chapter, in 2017 my wife and I formed a partnership with good friends and purchased a franchise location of Peace Love and Little Donuts in our local community. Besides the handful of small businesses my wife had created while being a stay at home mom, this was our first true leap into the world of entrepreneurship. This was our first experience where there was a significant financial risk on our end to start the business. I'm going to be honest, there were some real nerves when we chose to sign the five-year lease on a storefront space. Then things got even more real when the checks started flowing out for all the various equipment purchases and necessary construction costs. For my wife this day of graduating to the next level of entrepreneurialism was a day long overdue. For me it was a day I never saw coming. I always assumed, even in college, that I would always work for other people. I certainly envisioned myself to be successful someday; but that vision of success always entailed working to grow and develop someone else's dream. But now things were shifting in my life. Shifting from working diligently to increase my value in an organization to increasing the value of an organization, my organization.

The months prior to opening were a whirlwind, especially for my wife. She was in-charge of managing the build out of our space with our general contractor who just happened to be her father. Since everyone in my wife's family are involved in the construction business it was a natural fit for her to take the lead during the construction phase. We both had an idea that things would get busier and busier the closer we got to opening our doors, other franchise owners gave us fair warning of how hectic things would get. The franchise was very open about the time and effort which would be needed to open our doors to the public. However, even with all this warning and information, we still underestimated what it would really be like.

My wife was taking calls all day long. There were issues with our permits. There were issues with the township's inspector. There were issues with the plumbing, electrical, and fire prevention. There were late nights and early mornings. Once I had to go to our location at 2 am, yes 2 o'clock in the morning, to open the doors for some people to clean a shaft for our ventilation hood! There was a ton of rescheduling because of having to handle unexpected problems. Subcontractors wouldn't commit to time frames. When they did commit to being done by a certain time they would inevitably change or extend. We were spending our nights and weekends doing what we could to save money with construction costs. We did the painting and the cleaning. We picked up and delivered heavy equipment purchased off Craig's List. I personally installed and wired the in-ceiling speakers. (The fact that the same speakers I installed are still working and hanging in the ceiling tiles is proof to me that God actually does exist.) The list goes on and on.

> "When is this going to get easier?"

If you have ever started your own business, I'm sure you have similar stories. Well, the mounting stress and pressure was mostly focused and hanging on the shoulders of my wife. One night I was driving in my car and my cell phone rang. It was my wife. There wasn't any pleasantries or greetings, just straight into the frustration du jour. To be honest, I can't even remember what the exact situation was which was raising her blood pressure and prompting her call. But I can recall it sounding something like this, "Why can't ABC Plumbing Company ever do what they say they will do? They told me they were going to install widget 1 by Saturday and here we are on Wednesday still waiting. XYZ Flooring Inc., can't start until those guys are finished and I can't even schedule the work until I know a date." This type of banter went on for another minute or so. Then, she hit me with the real issue behind the frustration, "Mark, when is this going to get better? When is this going to get easier?"

I have known my wife for over 18 years. We dated and were engaged for 3 years and have been married for 15 years on top of that. I know when to listen to her and be supportive. I also know when to correct and challenge her thinking. I decided to go with the latter, although I wasn't sure how she would react to me challenging her mindset in this exact moment. I didn't want to overwhelm or add to her frustration, but I also knew that this moment's learning opportunity was too great to pass up.

So, as she finished by saying, "When is this going to get easier?" I quickly interjected and firmly responded with, "It's not! It's not going to get easier Amy!" I paused. I waited for her to speak. It seemed like forever. I knew at this point my words were sinking in. They pierced through the wall of her emotions and got to her heart. A few more moments passed.

"Keep going," she said.

"You have to see all this work, effort, and pressure as an opportunity. All this isn't destroying you, but preparing you for the next business, the next store, the next idea. Pain creates strength."

"Keep going," she said again. I obliged.

"If you only see everything that needs done as list of tasks needing checked off, then next time we want to do something you will struggle and stress all over again. Don't approach it like that, approach it as an opportunity to get stronger, smarter, and better. Whenever I work out my muscles are stretched and torn by the weights and my effort. Then the next day I'm sore and in pain. But that pain is temporary and is a sign my muscles are growing and getting stronger. The same thing goes for you. This process has been painful, absolutely. But the pain will produce a stronger, better you that is able to handle more weight the next time. What if this is the smallest thing we ever start? You'll look back and be grateful on what you learned and developed over the past few months. There is purpose to all the pain, it's our future."

"It's not going to get easier…"

A few more moments of silence.

"Thanks, Hun. I needed that." Then, she hung up the phone.

There are a number of moments I can remember over 18+ years of knowing my wife where I have been so extremely proud of my wife. The list is topped by each time she delivered one of our three children. She was tough and determined. She once taught a lesson on personal finances to our church. She was eloquent, engaging, and confident. She once walked into a consignment store, unsolicited, and sold hundreds of dollars of product. She was personable and convincing. But that conversation driving in my car, that one is up there for me. How does a simple conversation rank up there with children being born and helping others achieve financial freedom? She was humble and teachable. She was eager to learn and grow even with me being the one doing the teaching. (As a side note, many times it's most difficult to take tough advice from the people closest to us. Don't be too proud to accept advice from the people who love you the most.) She didn't allow her emotions to rob her of what was developing on the inside of her. She chose to be teachable instead. She allowed herself to be refined by the process and turned a frustrating situation that had the potential to be destructive into something that was constructive.

FIRE OR RUST

Fire or Rust. Pick one. What do I mean by that? If we want to improve, if we want to grow and develop then we must be willing to "go through the fire". Fire refines but excuses extinguish. Let me clarify. The Bible says in Proverbs 27:17, "as iron sharpens irons, so one person sharpens another." Anytime something needs to be sharpened there has to be friction in order to make it happen. If you aren't willing to experience a little bit of friction, then you will develop excuses which will extinguish any chance of growth or improvement. You can have some friction or remain covered in rust, you choose. You can experience a little bit of heat or remain dull. Which will it be?

> "Fire refines but excuses extinguish."

Friction creates heat. My wife allowed me to create some friction by challenging her during a difficult moment. The friction wasn't to destroy her but to sharpen her. This friction sharpened her skills. It sharpened her thinking. It sharpened her focus. Ultimately it made her more effective and valuable. What good is a dull knife when something needs cut? Not much. If a knife lost its ability to cut it would be useless. It would carry no value. We should aim to keep ourselves sharp by allowing friction, or heat, to teach us and mold us.

Let me say something that could be both encouraging and discouraging, if there isn't heat then there isn't any improvement. If you are currently experiencing some heat from a situation, then you should be encouraged because you're currently being sharpened. You're being made more effective and useful. That can also be discouraging if you are the type of person who avoids heat at all costs. Some people avoid being challenged or experiencing discomfort like it's the Bubonic Plague. If the situation is easy, then chances are you aren't going to grow or develop from it. How could you become sharper unless friction is present?

PRESSURE PRODUCES

Do you know the other attribute of sharpening that needs to exist for something to become sharper? Pressure. Actually, pressure is a prerequisite for friction. There aren't any sparks unless there is friction. There isn't any friction unless there is pressure. The appropriate amount of pressure from a sharpening stone is what starts the sharpening process. Now, if you apply too much pressure, you'll ruin the blade. But if there isn't enough pressure, then you won't have any impact or generate the right result. Appropriate pressure. Appropriate pressure won't destroy you, but it also won't allow you to remain the same. The appropriate amount of pressure is beneficial. It should be sought out. When the appropriate amount of pressure is applied to your life you become sharper and it increases your value to the world.

> "When the appropriate amount of pressure is applied to your life you become sharper and it increases your value to the world."

Let's get back to the story of opening our donut franchise. Finally, after lots of hard work, coordination, and planning our opening day was within sights. May 17th, 2018 finally came. It was our first day of being open to our community. Now, during the research and planning process, all of our contacts and resources were telling us the same thing: Your problem won't be how to attract customers, it will be how to keep employees. Other franchise owners and even the corporate franchise directors themselves were setting the same expectation and speculating we will have their same problems. "You will quietly and discretely open your doors one day and word will get out quickly to the masses. Somebody will walk by and see your "OPEN" sign. They will come in and buy some of your delicious donuts. Then, this mystery person will Tweet, share on Instagram and post on Facebook that your store is open. Within minutes there will be a line out the door with new customers eager to try your donuts. Hundreds and thousands will flock like moths to a flame.

Well, maybe I'm exaggerating that last part a bit, but the truth is we were convinced that for the first two to three months we wouldn't be able to make donuts fast enough. Then, we were told that all the high school and college-aged kids you just hired will get stressed out by the long lines and quit. You will end up having to work extra shifts to keep the doors open and basically be living at your store."

Um. Except it didn't happen quite like that.

We were busy from day one, but not overwhelmed. The lines were long at times, but never completely unmanageable. As for our employees, we didn't have any quit. In fact, some of them were fighting over who was given any available extra shifts. The sixty to ninety day "honeymoon period" ended up being more like 30 days instead.

We had a different set of problems than what we were expecting. We were anticipating difficulties in finding, hiring, and retaining hard working employees. We were anticipating problems in keeping up with the volume of people. In reality, we faced other problems, other pressures. We faced other unforeseen, unplanned pressures. Full disclosure, things weren't horrible. I don't want to make it seem like we couldn't pay our bills or had to keep pumping money into the business. It wasn't that bad, but sales weren't where we wanted or expected them to be. Guess what that created? Pressure and friction. Appropriate pressure and sharpening friction.

> "Pressure can create or destroy. Pressure is both dynamic and explosive."

Pressure can be two faced. It can both create and destroy. Pressure is the creative force that forms diamonds out of coal. However, pressure is also the destructive force within a bomb that can level a building. Pressure can create or destroy. Pressure is both dynamic and explosive. Pressure can be both good and bad. Pressure brings out both the best and the worst in people. With pressure some people perform at their best while others crumble under the weight of the situation.

READING YOUR PRESSURE GAUGE

In order for you to find success, whether it means starting something completely new or striving to increase with what you are currently doing, you have to answer the following questions regarding your own pressure gauge. How much pressure can you handle? Is the pressure you are experiencing at an appropriate level? We all must accurately determine how we react, respond and resolve varying levels of pressure in our lives. Once we understand our limitations then work to maintain an appropriate amount of regular pressure. Not too much that it overwhelms, but enough that keeps pushing us forward.

So, what do we do about the mounting and building pressure? How do we deal with it? What I've found is that our actions are like opening a valve to release the pressure mounting inside of us. Conversely, our inaction (doing nothing) just lets the pressure build and build.

Our efforts should not be entirely focused on how we can eliminate pressure in our lives. We should also be working to improve how we respond and manage pressure. With our donut franchise we had to accept the reality of our situation and allow the pressure and heat of business ownership to sharpen our ability to market and advertise to our community. It sharpened us creatively. We had to acknowledge the facts and then respond appropriately. You can't ignore reality or the facts. That's just being ignorant. You must address the facts with thoughtful reaction and proactive plans. Our reaction to seeing lower sales figures was cost reduction. We immediately began to identify hours where we were staffed too heavily. We began to closely monitor how much product we were ordering from our suppliers. We reacted by slowing the outflow of our finances.

"Your ability to handle pressure should grow over time."

However, reactive solutions will not prevent future issues from occurring which is why it's critical to both react to the immediate and plan for the future. So, our proactive plan was to be more focused, diligent, and creative with our marketing and advertising. We decided to spend more time developing creative social media programs and ads. We spent time to work on catering sales and marketing around holidays with coupons and promotions. Sometimes, when pressure is building the best thing to do is take a deep breath, develop a plan, and get to work.

PRESSURE SHOULD IMPROVE

How do you improve the way you handle pressure? Act. You might deal poorly under intense or even moderately pressure-packed situations; it doesn't always have to be that way. If you don't apply any pressure you can't be refined, if you apply too much it can be destructive. Your ability to handle pressure should grow over time.

It grows as we grow.

In 2003 I was a junior at Geneva College. That December I went to the winter formal dance with my then girlfriend, now wife. We went with a bunch of our other friends and were having a great time. The dance was held in a ballroom at a nearby hotel. Since Geneva is a small college outside of Pittsburgh there were only about 150 students who came to the dance. As a result, our ballroom was one of three being rented that evening by the hotel. The ballroom which happened to be adjacent to our ballroom was being rented by some company for their employee Christmas party. Amy and I were having a good time dancing and laughing with our friends when we noticed our college group slowly getting smaller. I didn't think anything of it until my best friend came rushing back into our ballroom. "Mark and Amy, you guys gotta come follow me. Some of the track team went into that company's Christmas party next door and are dancing with all these old people. It's hilarious. Let's go!"

We followed my buddy Josh towards this other party. When we turned the corner into this separate ballroom, I saw a mixture of young and old. It looked exactly like most wedding receptions. There was a large circle already formed and people were taking their turn in the middle to show off their best moves. Everything was pretty typical and as you might expect, uncoordinated people dancing mediocrely. Then, things got crazy. One of guys on the track team, an All-American hurdler, made his way to the middle. He did a short break dance then jumped into the air and landed a perfect split. Everybody went nuts. The crowd was cheering and yelling. It was by far the best display of moves the whole night.

Now, who in their right mind was going to follow that? Answer, someone who wasn't in his right mind. Someone who was really, really drunk. So, this older guy, super wasted and super confident from his super drunkenness, yells out, "You like that? Well watch this!" Spoiler alert, this does not end well for our mystery man. This guy in his mid-40s steps out into the middle of the circle. He does a few offbeat and uncoordinated dance moves circa the early 90's. He then jumps as high as he can (which wasn't very high) and tries to do a split just like my athletic, limber, incredibly flexible college hurdler friend. Now, I must hand it to the guy, he sure did give his all out on the dance floor. Unfortunately, his best effort was not good enough on this night. As soon as he hit the floor his eyes almost popped out of his head, he grabbed his legs and started screaming. He kept screaming, "My groin! I can't move! Someone call an ambulance!" His inebriated mind wrote a check that his groin flexibility couldn't cash.

We all quickly left this company's ballroom laughing uncontrollably. Sure enough, about 15 minutes later some medics showed up with a stretcher. They lifted this man onto it and wheeled him into the back of an ambulance. To this day, I'm not completely sure if that man ever walked again. Maybe the damage to his groin might was too extensive to repair. I may never know. I'm joking about him never walking again, but I would bet a lot of money that the mystery guy sure did have weeks and weeks of recovery from one moment of incredible foolishness.

> "…you had better put in the time stretching yourself and preparing if you want to develop abilities you don't currently possess."

There are a few takeaways from that story. The first lesson is that drinking will make you do dumb things. It will make you do dumb things that will make it impossible to walk the next day. Don't do dumb things. The second lesson is that you had better put in the time stretching yourself and preparing if you want to develop abilities you don't currently possess.

See, the All-American hurdler was flexible. Actually, to put it more accurately, he was extremely flexible. He was incredibly flexible. But here's the key, his flexibility did not come by accident. It was solely because he consistently spent a lot of time stretching and building his strength. His muscles were developed and loosened through hours of practice and painful stretching. There is no shortcut around this process. Ask that guy who left on a stretcher.

BE FLEXIBLE

Are you willing to stretch yourself so you can develop a skill or ability? Are you willing to spend the hours stretching and building upon yourself to reach a level of success which you've yet to experience? Are you willing to refine yourself through friction and appropriate pressure? I hope the answer is yes.

Our own personal growth and personal development will determine the growth, and rate of growth of our professional and business endeavors. We have to grow in order to impart growth. We must improve and develop in order to pass that along to our teams.

The Bible says Zechariah 4:10, "do not despise the days of small beginnings, for the Lord rejoices to see the work begin." This verse communicates a few things to me. The first thing it communicates is that starting small isn't a bad thing. God rejoices to see people headed to their unique purpose and destiny, even if it starts out with small steps. The second thing the verse communicates is that we should expect for our businesses and influence to grow. The Bible uses the phrase "small beginnings" because the assumption is that it will only be small in the beginning.

> "We have to grow in order to impart growth. We must improve and develop in order to pass that along to our teams."

The third thing this verse communicates is that the time frame of our small beginnings is measured in days. It doesn't say, "the years of small beginnings" or even "the decades of small beginnings." The time frame used to depict the length of time that we should be "small" is only days. The time frame used to describe the length of time that our uniqueness should be small is only days.

HAVE URGENCY

We need to nurture our uniqueness but with urgency. We need to grow our skills and abilities swiftly. Don't delay. Don't put it off. Why the rush? Because, the faster you grow, the faster your business will grow. The faster you can develop and improve, the faster you'll put yourself in a place where you are ready for promotion. Why? When you grow and develop personally you raise the ceiling on your potential.

Each of us, right now are limited by ceilings in our lives. Our current leadership capacity is limited by a ceiling. Our current skill set is limited by a ceiling. Our current emotional intelligence is limited by a ceiling. As you increase your leadership skills you raise the roof and create space to climb higher. The same goes for our skills set and emotional intelligence. As you raise the ceiling in these areas your business, family and workplace will reap the benefit from the effort you put into your own growth pace. Some people will live their lives as one-story ranch homes while others will be like skyscrapers. The difference? Their own investment into themselves.

Refine yourself at whatever cost at each and every opportunity. Don't run from friction. Don't avoid a little bit of heat. Don't flee from appropriate pressure. Instead allow these tools to sharpen you so you become more effective. Allow these tools to chip off any rust so you become more flexible. As you become more flexible you increase your value.

CHAPTER 7 – BE DARING AND DO IT!

Henry Ford once said, "If you always do what you've always done, then you'll always get what you've always got." I like that quote. It's not all that elegant or poetic, but it gets the job done. It sounds like it might have even come from a Pittsburgher. It's tough and to the point. As a young boy I always thought of myself as a risk-taker. I am a middle child with an older sister and a younger sister. They were never too interested in playing sports with me during long summer days so I would have to create games to play by myself when my neighborhood friends weren't around. I remember one game in particular that was a favorite of mine in the summertime. The game consisted of bashing a tennis ball off our garage door as I played a pretend tennis match in my head. Inevitably, because I wasn't Andre Agassi, and was in fact 12 years old, I'd miss the brick above the garage door and the tennis ball would go on the roof of the house and roll into a gutter.

At this point I had two options. Option one was to leave the tennis ball in the gutter and find something else to entertain me. Option two was to go inside the house, take off my shoes, go up to my room, take the screen out of the window, climb out my window, put my shoes back on so I wouldn't burn my feet on the hot shingles, retrieve the ball, climb back into the house through the window, put the window screen back in place, take my shoes back off, go down stairs, put my shoes back on and return to playing. Exhausting huh? So, in an effort for.... "efficiency" I found a much faster way to retrieve my displaced ball and return to my pretend match. What I decided was the simpler process to getting back to having fun would be to simply jump off the 8-foot roof after I got the ball out of the gutter. I had an option, the bold way or the safe way. I chose bold. Contrary to what you might be anticipating this way never steered me wrong. Well, I guess I can't say that. The only time it didn't work out so great is when my little sister was with me and I forced her to jump off the roof with me. She was only eight years old at the time and not nearly as nimble as I. She laid on the ground holding her ankles and crying. She ended up being just fine but for a few minutes I thought for sure my dad was going to send me to military school or something.

What happened to that childlike boldness? No consideration of the risks. No pros and cons list. No weighing the options, just finding a soft spot in the grass and jumping.

GO AHEAD, JUMP

Go ahead and jump into your uniqueness. Go ahead and start moving towards your identified intersection. You have my permission. Consider how you are going to land, find a nice soft patch of grass, but definitely jump.

I want to encourage you to be daring and take the first step. For each person reading this book that probably means something a little different. Maybe it's looking at store front retail space for your business concept. Maybe it's starting a podcast and publishing the first episode to your social networks. Maybe it's enrolling in a class or attending a seminar to develop new skills or hone ones you already have. The most important thing isn't what the step is, the most important thing is taking action and creating movement.

Be bold. Be very bold.

Boldness is a common denominator often found in the hearts of men and women who are walking in their own uniqueness. Boldness to face critics. Boldness to make your life's work open to the public and the critics which will surely follow. Boldness to take a risk. Boldness to believe in yourself. You should try on some boldness. I promise it'll look good on you.

Let's go back to that same group of Israelites we've talked about in previous chapters. Do you remember when I mentioned that the spies who scouted the new land God was going to hand-over to the Israelites were filled with doubt, fear, and small-minded thinking? Well, we see that Joshua believed God and trusted God to do what He said He would do. In chapter 1 of the book of Joshua, God was giving Joshua instructions on what to do next and he told Joshua twice to "be strong and courageous". Then God reiterates the need for boldness and courage a third time and says in verse 9, "This is my command—be strong and courageous! Do not be afraid or discouraged. For the Lord your God is with you wherever you go."

God told Joshua to be strong. He told him to be courageous. This tells me that boldness and courage are both a choice and a possibility. If these weren't a choice, then God wouldn't have needed to command him to do be bold and courageous. This also tells me that boldness is possible. If it weren't possible for Joshua to be bold, then God would not have commanded him to do something which was impossible. So often people will decide that they are not bold or lack courage and indicate that it is not in their personality to have either one. "I'm just not a bold person, it's not my personality. I'm not very courageous, I'm not a risk-taker." God is saying, "No, no, no! Boldness and courage are possible traits for you live in today." Decide today, you will be bold and act courageously. You will choose boldness instead of timidity. You choose courage instead of fear.

> "Boldness is a common denominator often found in the hearts of men and women who are walking in their own uniqueness."

Often, we use our personality as a scapegoat to avoid addressing things that could be changed within us. What I mean by that is we will make the follow type of statements about ourselves, "I'm not a people person. I'm not a morning person. I'm not adventurous. I don't deal with change very well. I'm not a risk taker. I am a perfectionist. I am a control freak." We will often integrate statements like these as descriptions about our personalities. Except these aren't personality traits at all, each one of those statements are flaws within our character. Don't cement a character flaw as being permanent in your life by labeling it as a personality trait. Each one of those statements will make success more difficult to attain.

Do you remember what I said in chapter 1, "Anything you allow to define you will confine you."? Don't define yourself as being timid or shy. Instead, realize that you can be bold, it's possible. Instead, choose to be courageous. So, how? How do we become bold if it's not our tendency? What I've found, as a previously self-defining "non-risk taker", is that we can learn boldness in small steps. Start small. Learn to become comfortable in situation that used to make you uncomfortable. Start to seek out situations that will develop this part of your personality that might seem unnatural. You can do it!

4 TIERS OF LIVING

Every person on Earth lives within one of the following groups, or tiers, with regards to their thinking and mindset regarding their own life and circumstances. These groups are like a pyramid, meaning that the majority of people live in the bottom tier. As you climb the pyramid the number of people in each group become smaller and smaller and the air becomes rarified.

1. Complaining People

The base group of people, the bottom tier, are those who complain about their circumstances yet do nothing. This is the group with the highest population. I'm sure people like this are flooding to the forefront of your mind (hopefully you didn't immediately think of yourself). Why is this the largest piece of the pyramid? Because it's easy and convenient to complain. Complaining seems harmless, especially when the complaints aren't directed to specific people. However, nothing could be farther from the truth. Complaining is like a reverse magnet to growth and personal development. Complaining repels growth, promotion, and the motivation to develop personally. On top of that, complaining is also a repellent of other people. People usually don't desire to be around complainers and whiners. On a personal level, I actively try to avoid people who constantly complain. When I identify a person as being a complainer, it abruptly ends my pursuit for a deeper relationship with them. You can ask my wife; I can't stand being around constant complainers. When I am around such a person it feels like the lifeblood is being sucked from my veins.

Could that be a character flaw within me? Possibly. But I think it speaks to how complaining establishes a negative atmosphere and environment. Remember those Israelites who died in the desert? Their inability to stop complaining kept them complacent from further change and ultimately sealed their tragic fate to die in the desert. Don't die in a "desert" place in your life. Instead, reject complaining and move forward. Don't be a person that constantly and consistently complains. Complaining about it being too hot in the summer.

Complaining about it being too cold in the winter. Complaining about your boss, your co-workers, your spouse, your kids, your car, your house, your health, your weight.

2. **Lip Service Only People**

The second tier are those who complain about their circumstance, saying they want their own circumstance to change but ultimately do nothing. This group includes those people who have isolated what needs to change but, for whatever reason, don't ever allow their desire to transform their actions. Action is necessary. I hope you see that now as I have already encouraged you to act multiple times within this book. I've encouraged thoughtful actions through the consideration of your skills and passions. I've encouraged action by putting pen to paper and listing your skills and passions. Beliefs and convictions aren't enough. Desire isn't enough either. Action is a prerequisite for life change to happen. But because actions elude this group, these people will remain stuck with minimal life change. Remember this, complaints have never solved one problem since the beginning of time. Actions create solutions, complaining creates decay. An easy way to ensure your tomorrows are always like your yesterdays is to complain about today but do nothing different tomorrow.

3. **Partial Effort People**

The third tier is a group of people who say they want their circumstances to change, they have good intentions to change, and even implement a few actions. Unfortunately, this group does not implement enough changes, or they give up too quickly and ultimately, they stay where they are. I feel like this is the group that is most frustrating to stay stuck in. It's a group of people that have a proper vision, maybe even have an intersection identified loaded with value to pursue. However, their commitment, perseverance, and dedication aren't equal to challenges that might present themselves and they give up and quit.

You could read countless stories of people who are immensely successful who went through a large number of rejections and failures until they ultimately encountered their success. Walt Disney, you know him, right? The guy who built an amusement empire amassing thousands of acres of property and unbelievable wealth after being rejected 302 times for financing. Could you imagine having been rejected 283 times in a row and yet trying again for the 284th time?

Sylvester Stallone's screenplay for a movie titled "Rocky" was rejected 1,500 times. The list goes on and on. What if your next meeting is the one where you experience the breakthrough you've been dreaming about for years? What if your next idea or pursuit is the one on which you build a generational legacy. Don't you owe it to your family, your children, yourself to see your uniqueness through as far as you can possibly take it?

> "... people who say they want their circumstances to change and they implement whatever needs to happen, for as long as it needs to happen, in order to see the change actually and fully manifest"

4. Do What It Takes People

The fourth and top tier is a group of people who say they want their circumstances to change and they implement whatever needs to happen, for as long as it needs to happen, in order to see the change actually and fully manifest. This is my belief for you. This is the group you are in starting now. You are bold and courageous. You are skilled and passionate. Your future is worth the effort and energy. Your vision will come to pass. Now grab tightly to your uniqueness and refuse to quit fighting for your future. Refuse to give up if things aren't going as planned. Refuse to throw in the towel if you encounter resistance or difficulty. Be bold. Be courageous. Be tenacious and fearless.

What group are you in? Most people have no problem complaining about their predicament. Can you move past the problem and into action? Can you see past your issue and see the unique potential inside of you?

STEPPING OUT OF THE BOAT

One day Jesus told his disciples to get into a boat and make their way towards the other side of a lake as he was going to stay behind and pray. The disciples, some of whom were experienced, professional fisherman found themselves in the middle of a lake inside of a terrible storm. They were fighting against the wind and waves which were pushing them in the opposite direction of where they wanted to go. Have you ever felt that way; like the Earth and everything in it were resisting your effort? As these men were doing their best to make progress, but ultimately going nowhere, one man decided to try something different, something bold. A man named Peter saw Jesus walking on the water with seemingly no issue. Peter had a chance to take a bold step into the water, into the waves, into the storm, into uncertainty, and try a different way through the storm. What always irked me about this story is that many people give Peter a hard time because he begins to sink after a few steps when his focus changes from Jesus to the dangerous wind and waves. But here's my opinion, we don't know how many steps Peter took walking on top of pure H2O. Let's say it was ten steps, well that's ten more steps than I've ever taken, or you have ever taken. He had the boldness to step out of what he knew and into the unknown.

That story encourages me to take the first step off the boat. To step off something that seems so comfortable to me even if it isn't working. What is interesting is that these men were trained to operate a boat, yet the safest place for them was outside of what they knew and on the waves. Comfort is often the enemy of courage. Comfort and courage are often mutually exclusive. Soldiers who are courageous certainly wouldn't describe their conflicts which displayed their courage as comfortable situations. A preference to remain in something you perceive as comfortable will prevent you from living courageously and moving towards something new. It's time to get out of the boat. It's time to take the first step.

> "Comfort is often the enemy of courage."

The key is to start small and gain momentum. Start by taking small steps to towards your identified intersection. Begin by researching online, gathering information, and making connections. These first steps will either lead to a clear sign to stop and reassess the value of the intersection or the steps will lead you farther and farther down the path towards your destiny.

WHO IS BEHIND ME?

As you set out on your bold and courageous new adventure, be sure to have a select group of people in your life who can provide advice, correction, and mentoring. This is such an important consideration that people often fail to fully consider and implement. It can be dangerously easy to listen to voices of those who are already very close to us. These are not always the same people that are best to have as advisors. The people may not be our closest friends, our family members, or even spouses sometimes. I'm not saying that we should get out of these close relationships but reserve the role of an advisor for a very, very, VERY select group. Our inner circle should meet certain qualifications. Inner circle members should be positive, informed, and encouraging. Positive, Informed and Encouraging. Your closest confidants should have all three of these attributes.

They should be positive, not negative. Nothing is more deflating than telling someone your hopes and dreams and having that person respond sounding like Eeyore from Winnie the Pooh. Negative people will always focus on the obstacles, challenges, and problems and will usually end by surmising that this opposition is too large. Positive people don't just ignore the issues. Positive people might identify the same issues but will have a belief that you can conquer each challenge. "That might be hard, but you can do that." You want someone who is a "glass half full" kind of person.

Your inner circle should be informed. They should have some level of knowledge or be inclined to advise in a helpful manner. Try to identify people with relatable knowledge in the field you are interested in pursuing. They don't have to be experts, but at least familiar enough with the field to give some general guidance. Let me make a clear distinction on the difference between someone in your inner circle and someone who can provide expert advice. For example, if I was interested in starting an accounting firm then I would seek expert advice from someone in the industry or someone who has already succeeded in starting his or her own firm. Determine if this person is merely an advisor with expert knowledge or someone invited to the inner circle. That same person, who has seen their own success, may not necessarily be in my inner circle though. He or she could or could not be. Why? Because of the third attribute of being encouraging.

> "… don't do something stupid. Do something bold with thought and consideration."

Your advisors should be encouraging. People with expert knowledge may not be prone to be encouraging. They actually might be prone to dissuade you based upon their own personal experience or inadequacies. Each person in my inner circle need to be part of my personal cheerleading squad. So that when feelings of doubt creep into my mindset or if I feel overwhelmed with what needs accomplished, I have encouragers insulating my uniqueness. Encouraging people are easy to be around. There never seems to be a shortage of discouraging, "can't do it", negatively minded people wanting to give you their two cents. Find people who will encourage you to fight for your dreams. Find people who will encourage you by reminding you of your skills and passions. These people make all the difference.

Despite the story I used at the beginning of this chapter, don't confuse bold for carelessness. In fact, I would even say that 12-year-old me jumping off an eight-foot roof wasn't careless. I was old enough and agile enough to handle the fall. It was boldly efficient. However, what was careless was making my eight-year-old sister jump. That was stupid. Hear me, don't do something stupid. Do something bold with thought and consideration. It wasn't careless when Peter stepped off the boat and into the water. He was bold and daring. I wonder if some of the other disciples tried to talk him out of stepping off. I wonder if they didn't have a positive attitude towards Peter's plan. I wonder if they weren't informed like Peter because they didn't see Jesus walking on the water for themselves. Maybe the others didn't hear Jesus' voice calling out for Peter to walk towards him. I wonder if they weren't encouraging Peter to do something bold and amazing.

IT'S UP TO YOU

Be bold. Be courageous. You will never know what could happen until you make it happen. The Israelites, while in the desert, knew very well their position in life. They knew what their lives would be like in the desert climate they were currently living in. They lived in the desert as wanderers. They had been doing it for years and I'm sure to some degree grew to be comfortable in that naturally uncomfortable environment. What they didn't fully understand is just how awesome of a land God had handpicked for them. They tasted some of the fruit and saw some of the property, but their lack of boldness and courage prevented them from seeing their family, children, and grandchildren live and thrive in the abundant place God wanted them to experience. Start moving towards your uniqueness with boldness and courage. Start moving towards your identified and valuable intersection boldly through research, investigation, and planning.

Towns and cities are a vast network of intersections. Where there are intersections, there are usually people. The intersection of your skills and talents is a town called Uniqueville. However, Uniqueville's population is only 1. You are the only resident. You are the only citizen. No two people are both skilled and passionate in the same way. Knowing how we have been uniquely made, discovering what is inside of us, which is special, valuable is not the end of the exercise. So, if you are the only citizen well then, I have good news, you're the mayor. You're the boss. You make all the decisions. You get all the credit, but you also bear the responsibility for all the blame. Do you see the dichotomy? All the good and all the bad falls back on your shoulders.

It is time to take full responsibility for your life. No more excuses, no more blaming. You are where you are because of what you have done with what you were given. The blame game is just about the easiest thing to do in life. Blaming others is internally the path of least resistance. It's right up there with throwing pity parties, being lazy, and not taking any risks. The blame game is one of our Potential Trap's most beloved tactics to keep us where we are. We blame our upbringing. We blame our education. We blame our intelligence. We blame our location. We blame our spouse, our children, our parents. We blame everyone except for the one person mostly responsible: ourselves!

At the root of every issue in our lives in the same thing, us. You are the common denominator of every problem. But wait, there's good news. Since every issue has a similar root, one fix fixes all issues. If you fix you, then you fix just about everything. Stop blaming and start addressing.

Start something. Get on the move. Be willing to fight for your dreams. Make the decision to be bold. Make the choice to be courageous. Take that first step towards your unique intersection with confidence.

Over the next few chapters I want to discuss a few of the emotions and feelings that we often must conquer in order to keep our momentum and keep our progress moving forward. Three factors that we have to address and defeat in order to realize our dreams: fear, insecurity, and hesitation.

SECTION 3 – OVERCOMING SPEED BUMPS AND ROADBLOCKS

CHAPTER 8 – THE FEAR FACTOR

Fear is the first factor that we will most likely face. The fear factor. No, I don't mean anything like that show in the early 2000's with Joe Rogan. Do you remember that program? It was where people had to eat gross stuff or lay down in a tub of worms and whoever could last the longest or eat something disgusting the fastest would keep from being eliminated. Eventually someone would win something like $100 and an Olive Garden coupon for doing all this awful stuff (Full disclosure: I have no idea what they won. However, I can assure you that whatever relatively nominal prize they did receive wouldn't be worth it for me to go through those tests). No, this fear factor isn't anything quite that creepy. I am referencing the fear that raises up from time-to-time always with the worst-case scenario. What if this happens? What if you fail? What if you bankrupt your family? What if you start down the path of irreparable financial problems? What if this fear? What if that fear? We have a choice to either entertain and feed our fears or to starve them and keep moving.

SNEAKY SNAKES

A few years ago, I was cutting the grass in our backyard and my four-year-old daughter was playing nearby in her playhouse. While I was pushing the lawnmower, I felt a tug on my shorts. I shut off the engine and took my headphones out of my ears. Juli was shouting at me, "Daddy, there is a snake in my house. I saw a snake Daddy."

Now, I'm not super proud of what I did next. I glanced towards her playhouse, gave it a quick once over, and said, "There's no snake Juli. Go back and play." I put my headphones back into my ears and resumed cutting the grass.

Approximately 23.6 seconds later, Juli came running back to me, except this time she is much more animated about this alleged snake sighting. This time she was shouting louder and was sounding much more convincing that she did indeed see a snake.

"I swear Daddy I saw a snake. It was a sneaky snake and I swear I saw it! Come get it please, please, please, please get the sneaky snake. I'm not joking about the snake, Daddy!"

A little background is needed for this story's sake. In Juli's children's Bible, which we read to her most every night, the second story is about the first sin ever committed by Adam and Eve. It is called 'Sneaky Snake'. Therefore, every snake that Juli sees is a sneaky snake, and I'd tend to agree with her.

Back to the story, I began to carefully inspect the playhouse for this snake and I finally see it slithering between the wood slats on the playhouse steps mostly hidden by the steps themselves. I did what every tough, protective father would do, I yelled, "AMY!" Before you judge me, I didn't call for her to take care of the problem. I called for her to bring me a few necessary snake removal instruments which consisted of a grilling spatula and a hammer. While she delivered the tools, I kept a watchful eye on this unwanted intruder. I then used the snake removal kit to pry him out of the small space where he was trying to hide by use of my spatula. I must add; my initial plan was the use the grilling spatula to chop him in half. Don't try that method. It doesn't work at all, trust me.

After I got him out of the little crevice he was hiding in I laid him in the grass and pinned him to the ground with my trusty metal spatula. Then the sneaky, slimy, slithering snake got a few quick and deadly blows from the trusty hammer and was returned to the woods lifeless and dead. It was a great day. I was the hero. You might be wondering if I did all of this in plain sight of my daughters. Uh, absolutely I did. And their reaction, you might be wondering; they were pumped! My daughters were chanting, "Daddy! Daddy! Daddy killed the snake!" over and over. It was glorious. I can still hear it in my head, and it makes me smile. All was right in the world, and in my daughter's playhouse, once again.

What's the moral of the story? What does this have to do with overcoming the fear of starting something new? Here's the point: Don't let a sneaky snake of fear keep you from living in what is rightfully yours. That playhouse was given to my daughters by their father. That snake slithered into my daughter's house and its very presence brought fear with it and drove my daughter away. But my daughter did something that we fail to do as adults. She didn't accept her new fate, "Well I guess that snake lives in my house now and I'll just be homeless." Or even worse, "I guess I have to learn how to cohabitate with this snake now in my life. I'll probably have to deal with this snake the rest of my life." Instead she ran to her father who had the authority and ability to evict the snake and give her back possession of her house.

> "Feed your purpose and starve your fears. Starve them to death."

Feed your purpose and starve your fears. Starve them to death.

HANDLING SNAKES

You might be wondering why I had to kill the snake. Why couldn't I have just thrown him into the woods after catching him with my makeshift exterminator set? I'll tell you the reason. I wanted my children to see that the object which was bringing fear into their lives was dead. I wanted my daughters to know that all present fears, and any future fears, died with the lifeless, limp snake. I didn't want there to be any doubt in their minds that the snake issue could return. If I would have let that little guy live, then how easily could my daughters have been wondering when it would be slithering back? We can't cohabitate with our fear. We can't just live our lives and hope that fear stays in the woods far away from us. In fact, when fear, thoughts or emotions pop up into our minds there should be a part of us that immediately initiates a search and destroy mission. Don't feed your fear; instead, feed and nourish your purpose. Feed and nourish your identified intersection and bash the head of every snake of fear that tries to get you to retreat away from your full potential.

Anything you feed or nourish will grow. Anything you starve will die.

Meaning, anything you allow to remain in your life and nourish with your thoughts and words will multiply. You can see this principle in effect in our everyday lives. If you were to plant a new tree at your house you would have to continue to feed, nurture, and care for the tree well after planting the seed or base. You would have to water it and prune it to ensure it grows and develops properly. If you ignored the new tree, then it's chances of survival would diminish greatly. This even applies to our bodies, the more we feed ourselves the more we grow. I know this is a sad reminder for a lot of people. However, on the bright side the opposite is also true, anything you eradicate, starve, or reject will diminish and die off. The less we feed ourselves the more our bodies diminish in size. The less we water a new plant the greater the chance it has of dying.

"We can't expect for a mindset of continual fear to just magically stop because we dislike it's impact on our lives."

We can either feed our fears or starve them. We can't expect for a mindset of continual fear to just magically stop because we dislike it's impact on our lives. We must consciously and proactively starve that mode of thinking. You are on a seek and destroy mission; a mission to seek and isolate harmful habits and destroy them by identification and replacement. We identify fear and replace fear-filled thoughts with life-giving thoughts. We identify negativity and replace with positivity. These missions can happen night or day, rain or shine, weekends and weekdays. You are on active duty at home, at the office, at Wal-Mart, in traffic. Wherever the thought exists is where it dies of starvation.

DANGER AHEAD

Do you remember in the introduction where we discussed "traveler's fatigue"? Well, there is another aspect of traveling worth noting. Traveling can be dangerous. There are real things at stake with this book. Traveling from where you currently are towards your identified uniqueness does pose real risk. Our families. Our finances. This isn't something to take lightly but it also shouldn't hold us back. It's a calculated risk. I truly believe in God, as I mentioned in the beginning of the book. In the book of Matthew, Jesus describes the nature and character of God using the analogy of our fatherly relationships. Jesus teaches that good fathers on Earth, not absentee or abusive fathers, but loving, dedicated and present fathers would not put their children in harmful situations (by giving them a snake when they ask for fish) and they would ensure their growth (by giving them bread instead of a stone). Jesus caps off the teaching by stating, "If Earthly fathers know how to give their children good gifts, how much more will your Father in heaven give good gifts to those who ask him." (Matthew 7:9-11)

I'm lucky enough to have been raised by a very good father, and mother too. My father is supportive of my ideas. He uses his wisdom and understanding to guide me in my life. He prays for me and my family. He's not distant or disengaged. He's a great dad. But the Bible says that my earthly father's goodness towards me does not even remotely compare to my heavenly Father's goodness. As much as my earthly father loves me, his love doesn't hold a candle to God's love for me. The same goes for you too. The Bible says that perfect love cast out fear (1 John 4:18) and God's love towards us is perfect. When we know and fully understand the extent and power of God's love towards us it destroys fear from existing in us.

> "As God is good, His goodness extends to his children. That's me."

God is good.

This is an important principle to understand to extinguish fear, God is good. Plain and simple, God is good. As God is good, His goodness extends to his children. That's me. My heavenly father is also too good to lead me towards something harmful. That is why a connection to Him is so vital in this process. The Bible says that the steps of the righteous are ordered by God himself (Psalms 37:23). If he led me on a path towards destruction, then the Bible would contradict itself because God couldn't be simultaneously good natured and bad natured. God cannot be simultaneously loving and cruel towards His children. Now His leading can be, and is often, challenging but fear should not be involved. Be led by God, not fear.

Don't let fear dictate your direction in life.

Fear is a bully. Fear will try to push you around. Fear will push you out of your own potential if you allow it. Fear will try to make you give up before you even fight. Fear will make us freeze and then retreat away.

In the story of David and Goliath the Bible says in 1 Samuel 17 that David was sent to deliver food to his brothers at the battle lines. When David arrived, he heard Goliath, the Philistine giant and fiercest warrior, shouting at the Israelite army. He was shouting at the Israelites, intimidating them and instilling a feeling of fear. The Bible says that when the Israelite soldiers saw Goliath and heard his intimidating voice that they ran away in fear. Here's the thing, this army shouldn't have been retreating at all! They should have been advancing against Goliath to conquer him. They shouldn't have been running away from him, they should have been charging towards him. That was their destiny. But instead they allowed fear to dictate their action and direction which resulted in them running scared.

> "Fear will try to make you give up before you even fight."

Then, David arrived on the scene. I love how David did everything different than the trained soldiers whose job was to fight and advance. The army ran away from Goliath, but David ran towards him. The army didn't respond to Goliath's shouting, but David answered back to quiet him. The army didn't defeat him, but David won the battle.

Fear bullies us into inaction. Fear tells us all the reasons why something won't work out, why something will fail, why we will fail. Fear tries to speculate all the possible outcomes and ramifications of our "sure" failure. I'd bet that most people have encountered this feeling before in life. Right before you sign a document to start a business, fear invades. Right before you enroll in night classes to change careers, fear slithers into your mind.

3 TYPES OF FEAR

There are a few specific fears that will try to infiltrate your mind in order to deter your direction. I'd like to talk about each one of these specific fears.

1. **The fear of failure.**

This fear will try to intimidate you through the mere speculation of how you would feel if your idea doesn't work out. This fear is primarily emotion based. What will your friends think? What will your family think? If you fail, you'll be bankrupt, and your family will be living on the streets. If you fail, everyone around you will be talking about you and mocking you. It uses these strong emotions to intimidate and prevent us from action.

When I hear stories of people I knew in high school or college who took a risk and did something outside of normal, my reaction is usually one of respectful admiration. I admire them for pursuing a dream and taking a risk. I've often thought about if I would do the same thing if I were in their shoes. The fear of failing is often an indication of a level of insecurity in ourselves and placing too much importance in our reputation with others. Here's an easy trick to dissolve this fear. Often the fear of failure will pose the internal question, "What if?"

> What if...your business fails, and you are in financial problems?
>
> What if...your failure puts stress on your marriage?
>
> What if...your children only see you as a failure?

Instead of allowing the "What if" questions to haunt our minds and thoughts, add "... I don't" immediately after the "What if". So now it reads like this,

> What if I don't...start that business?
>
> What if I don't...write that book on my mind and my family just stays at the same level?
>
> What if I don't...take a risk on an idea a friend had for a new business?

Do you see how just a simple modification to the fear-based question puts a whole new spin on the negative, fear-based emotion. Now it's not negative, it's positive. Now it's not speculating the worst, it's encouraging us to think about what we might miss out on if we don't take the risk. Wayne Gretsky famously said, "you miss 100% of the shots you don't take." Don't let the fear of failure convince to never take a shot.

2. **The fear of wasting time.**

This fear will tell you that your idea is stupid. Or it will tell you that your idea is a good one, but you certainly couldn't do it and it will be a huge waste of time, money, and resources. I heard Bishop T.D. Jakes tell a story about his son dealing with this fear when considering if he should enroll in a school for music production after he finished high school. Bishop Jakes said that his son was worried about going down a career path that wasn't the best for him and that it would ultimately be a waste of his time and youth. Bishop Jakes advice to his son was this, even if this (music production) isn't the "thing" for you, it will be the "thing" that leads to the "thing". Meaning, our purpose in life is often determined through a series of events that build upon one another.

Very few people step directly and immediately into their long-term purpose. Apple had many products fail horribly before they found their niche within the technology market. Actors rarely start their career in leading or career defining roles. Denzel Washington's first role wasn't Malcom X or The Pelican Brief, not even close. In fact, the roles for those movies were in 1992 and 1993, respectively, about fifteen years after IMDB documents his acting career beginning in 1977. I wonder how he dealt with the successes and failures of beginning a career in Hollywood. Fifteen years of rejections and disappointments constantly trying to infiltrate your mindset of positive thinking. I wonder how close, if ever, he was to giving up and trying something more ordinary. Instead, with the added benefit of hindsight, you can see how one role led to another, led to another, led to connections and important friendships.

> "Nothing is wasted, nothing is discarded."

The Bible tells us the following in Romans 8:28, "And we know that God causes everything to work together for the good of those who love God and are called according to His purpose for them." I love that scripture. It's a constant reminder that my faith and love for God has put me into partnership with Him. This partnership document (the Bible) tells me that God will cause everything to work together for my good. Everything. The good things and bad things. It reassures me that nothing is a waste of time. That even instances that appear to be failure are really an important recipe in something good God is preparing for me. Nothing is wasted, nothing is discarded. So even if a business doesn't work out, I won't be the same at the end as the beginning. I'll be smarter, more educated, more experienced, and better positioned to succeed the next time.

3. **The fear of making the wrong choice or doing the wrong thing.**

This fear will tell you that the risk isn't worth the cost. However, the funny thing about fear is that it always neglects to mention the other cost involved in the decision. There are always two costs in every decision. The cost to do it and the cost to not doing it. Fear is awesome at getting us to consider the cost of doing something with a goal to ultimately discourage us enough from taking the first steps.

The cost of not doing something is also referred to in the business world as the 'opportunity cost'. Opportunity cost is the cost we pay of not doing something. So often we are only focused on what the cost will be if we do something. What will it cost me to open this storefront bakery? Well, we can figure out those costs like rent, build-out, equipment, products, decorating, and outfitting. What will it cost me to operate the business? We can figure out those costs too like our time, utilities, wages for employees, marketing, etc...

> "The fear mindset assumes failure and then is prevented from further investigation by paralyzed inaction. The person who thoughtfully decides not to pursue a new endeavor has been active the entire time."

I'm not AT ALL advocating that we neglect the consideration of the costs to do something, what I am advocating is that we do not neglect the consideration of the opportunity cost of not doing something. If the business is a success we could, then fill in the blank. We could pay off our house, pay for our children's college, or fund our retirement twice as fast. When making a decision, we need to properly determine both costs, the cost to do and cost not to do, then arrive at a decision with both costs in mind.

USING WISDOM

Fear is a paralyzing feeling. However, there is a difference between being paralyzed by fear and not doing anything as a result and thoughtfully passing on an opportunity. Even though the conclusions would seem to be the same, the processes are wildly different. The fear mindset assumes failure and then is prevented from further investigation by paralyzed inaction. The person who thoughtfully decides not to pursue a new endeavor has been active the entire time.

Let's use the idea of starting a landscaping business. This person would be actively identifying their particular scope of services to offer. They would have decided if they would be only cutting grass or offering a much broader list of services like creating bush beds, mulching, fertilizing, pest control, designing and planting landscapes, installing outdoor lighting, and so on. This person would have to determine the equipment needs of whatever service they ultimately decide to offer. They will probably need a truck, but will they also need a trailer, lawnmowers, weed eaters, hedge clippers, or a small backhoe as well. This person would have to identify where to market their services such as new developments, neighborhoods, business parks, or cemeteries. They would have to try to determine the need for their landscaping business in their area.

If the trend of these considerations results in a determination that the costs to open are greater than the cost to not open (opportunity cost) then this person would walk away from this endeavor. That person who did all the research wasn't paralyzed by fear but informed by action.

Don't allow a sneaky snake of fear to factor you out of your future.

Don't allow a sneaky snake of fear to drive you from the life which is rightfully yours.

Don't allow a sneaky snake of fear to keep you from living in your uniqueness.

Your uniqueness is too valuable to allow the emotion of fear to dominate your mind and discourage your actions. There is a '/' waiting for you on the other side of fear. Take out your grilling spatula and hammer so you can remove and kill each fear-filled thought attempting to prevent you from moving forward.

CHAPTER 9 – THE INSECURITY FACTOR

Insecurity is an odd human emotion. It's different than fear. Fear can be a result or a product of insecurity, but it's derived from a different root cause. Insecurity though, like fear, is one of the rock blocks trying to keep you from living in your full potential through the uniqueness inside of you.

I definitely would describe my teenage self as being insecure. It wasn't until my sophomore year in college that I was able to begin the process of truly becoming secure with who God created me to be. A lot of my adolescent insecurity was centered around a lack of self-confidence and self-worth. Since I lacked these things, I sought out external sources to provide these to my life instead of developing them within myself.

Here's a side note, don't look to outside sources to be your source of confidence, worth, joy, or peace. Culture cannot truly provide these to any person. Culture can offer counterfeits, but never the true thing.

So, back to 14-year-old Mark. Since I wasn't very confident in myself, I looked to my ability in sports to provide my confidence. I thought if I could prove to those around me that I was a great athlete then the popular crowd would like me more. Since I wasn't secure in my looks and physical body, I sought out attention from girls hoping that it would prove me to be handsome or good looking. The thing is, I had a great childhood with wonderful parents that loved me and supported me. I grew up going to church and loving Christ but seemingly always fought with insecurity in my mind. If I could just date the prettiest girl. If I could just hang around the most popular crowd. If I could do those things, then I must be worth something.

HOW INSECURITY WORKS

Fear comes into our minds and thoughts through external influences and circumstances. Fear, to me, is almost like a big black bear or ferocious lion. Fear intimidates from the outside and works its way inside. Insecurity is different. Insecurity is crafty. Insecurity starts on the inside and tries to work its way out of our minds and into our actions. Insecurity works from the inside out. Fear is overt. Insecurity is covert. Insecurity is working best when you don't even know it's there. For much of my adolescence I didn't realize how insecurity was poisoning my mind and thoughts. Here's the thing, I couldn't address the issue until I identified its presence inside of me. You can't evict something you haven't identified.

I remember exactly where I was when I finally addressed the insecurity and served it an eviction notice from my mind and thoughts. I was a sophomore at Geneva College sitting in a study room in the top floor of McCartney Library. I sat with a journal and my Bible (no iPads or smartphones back then) and talked with God. I made a decision and told God that I was done trying to establish my worth through a relationship with a girl. Instead, my worth was going to be based upon God's love for me. I told Him that I was done trying to build my confidence based upon my relationship status. My confidence would be based on who God created me to be. I told Him that I would instead begin drawing my worth and confidence from my status as a follower of Christ and son of God.

> "Insecurity works from the inside out. Fear is overt. Insecurity is covert."

After that evening in the library, it was only a few short weeks later that I began dating my wife. I believe that God had that relationship waiting for me until I was finally able to serve eviction to my insecurity. It's almost like he was waiting for me to be ready to enter the relationship as a secure man, not an insecure boy.

That was an incredible lesson I learned that night and over the next few weeks as my wife and I began dating. Here's the lesson: At no stage in life am I too young, too old, or too rich or poor to self-identify internal issues and serve eviction notices. Self-inventory is an underutilized weapon we have as adults. My faith provides routine and regular opportunity to scrutinize my actions, mindset, beliefs, and emotions. Why? Because through my faith I am being taught and shown how my life should look as I read about the example Jesus Christ set for me. My understanding of the ultimate example of Jesus challenges me to address anything keeping me from living as a better reflection of Him.

This is important to realize because you don't have to live tomorrow like you lived today, yesterday or any day before. Your thoughts and emotions don't have to dictate the terms of your life any longer. The only reason they dictate your life now is because you let them live in the space of your mind. Get them out! Start handing out eviction notices right now.

I want to illustrate how insecurity can be a wall preventing you from further progress towards your potential. Insecurity will limit your belief in yourself by making an opinion statement loosely grounded in fact. Here's what I mean:

> You are too small to be a good soccer player.
> You aren't smart enough to get the best job.
> You aren't funny enough to have cool friends.
> You didn't go to the right school.
> You're too broke to start that business.
> You don't have the strength or will power to overcome that issue.

Have you ever heard thoughts like this in your mind? Insecurity is the common denominator running through them all. How do we evict our insecurities?

DEVLOPING SECURITY

We must learn to become comfortable in our own skin. We must learn to become confidently comfortable with what we are skilled at doing instead of focusing on what we aren't so skilled at doing. This is the dangerous comparison game. Often, we compare ourselves with others and feel insecure by comparing our weaknesses to other's strengths. When I married my wife, I married into a family of construction contractors. My wife's father is a contractor. Her grandfather was a contractor and her great-grandfather was also a contractor. Now there is a fourth generation in the construction business as her brothers are both in the industry. I grew up with a father who was also an accountant, not a contractor. Not even a little bit of a contractor.

During our first few years of marriage I so frequently felt insecure about my inabilities working with my hands. Instead of focusing on my strengths, skills, and abilities, I was focused on my inadequacies compared to other's strengths. The comparison game is a game we so frequently lose. As I grew more confidently comfortable in my own skin, my insecurity in someone else's strength gave way to security in my strengths. No longer was I concerned that I didn't know what my in-laws knew. No longer was I embarrassed by not having certain abilities. Now my focus was on my skills.

> "Becoming confidently comfortable in our own skin is the process of informing our minds of our uniqueness."

Information evicts insecurity. Correct and truthful information will evict and eviscerate insecurity. Becoming confidently comfortable in our own skin is the process of informing our minds of our uniqueness. Evicting insecurity is informing our mind that we have unique intersections of value and refusing to let comparisons dominate our thinking. Let's review and evict some of the most prevalent insecurities we face one-by-one.

TYPES OF INSECURITY

Insecurity #1: I'm not smart enough.

Response: Living in your full potential is not dependent upon us knowing everything or being brilliant. However, often our full potential is dependent upon us being experts in one or two areas. Even people who say to themselves, "I'm too dumb or stupid", are very knowledgeable in some area. Chances are that area might be fantasy football, Facebook videos, or something that has no value or purpose. We can overcome this insecurity through the acquisition of information related to the area of our uniqueness. Meaning, put down the TV remote and learn something useful. In this incredible information age, there are no longer any excuses for ignorance. Not with YouTube and Wikipedia being accessible from our pockets twenty-four hours a day. We must make a choice to educate and inform ourselves, not about everything, but about something we have specifically identified which has value.

Many people come out of high school or college with this "I'm too dumb." mindset because they weren't successful in learning a subject that they weren't interested in, weren't inclined or weren't skilled to learn in the first place. Don't allow insecurities, which started because you struggled at geometry, impede your confidence at being a great plumber. Does the fact that you stunk at chemistry mean you can't own an advertising agency? Start learning and begin to educate yourself. Start with subjects related to your skills or passions. Start with topics that will move you towards seeing your unique intersection become reality. Often time people aren't too stupid, they are just too uninformed. Those are vastly different things. Not being smart enough will limit a person's capability to retain information. Being too uniformed only means that a person hasn't attempted to consume enough information. Be willing to put in the time to learn. It could be learning a new skill with your hands. It could be learning a new skill on a computer. It could be learning to develop better leadership skills. Inform yourself and watch insecurity vanish.

"Start learning and begin to educate yourself. Start with subjects related to your skills or passions."

Insecurity #2: I'm too inexperienced.

Response: Everybody must start somewhere, and everyone has started somewhere. Every successful CEO, entrepreneur, or risk taker was inexperienced at some point in time. Do you think Bill Gates knew how to run a successful software company before starting Microsoft? No, he didn't. He knew how to make a product and the rest was on-the-job training. Inexperience is only temporary. Inexperience only gets resolved by doing the very thing you are too insecure to do. It sounds silly when you think of it like this: insecurity tells us NOT to do something and remain inexperienced. The only way to become experienced is to gain experience by doing. If we would take that step of faith, be willing to learn and grow as we go, then inexperience quickly becomes experience. I've had that insecurity trying to infiltrate the firewall of my mind by using my inexperience as an author against me. "Why are you writing a book? What do you know about writing? Who would want to read that?" Honestly, the worst thing to do with insecurities is to leave them unanswered.

I decided to answer the questions my insecurity was posing in my head. My responses to my insecurities were honest and direct.

"Why am I writing this book?"
Because I want to.

"What do I know about writing?"
Letters form words, words form sentences, sentences form paragraphs and paragraphs form pages. Be authentic and show your personality, the rest I will learn as quickly as I can.

"Who would want to read this?"
At least myself and my wife. I am also pretty sure my parents and close friends will all buy a copy. That's about ten guaranteed book sales.

"How will you ever gain experience or credibility."
I will gain experience by starting the endeavor and creating my own experience. My credibility will come with consistency over time.

See how simple that is? We don't have to over complicate this process. When your mind or emotions pose a question to push you towards insecure thinking just respond with the simple, direct truth. After answering those questions in my mind, then the process didn't seem so overwhelming or scary. My responses re-grounded my feet into my identified uniqueness and put my vision back into focus.

Insecurity #3: I'm too broke.

Response: You might be too broke to do everything you want to do, but you're not too broke to do something. Here's the facts, money does matter. It does. It matters when you'd like to start a new idea and need cash to get it going. It matters when you are trying to publish a book as a first-time author. Money matters when you are trying to start a side job. But here's a lie, you need a significant amount of money to do something significant. Here's the truth, you can START something significant with what you have even if it's only a little.

The list of Fortune 500 companies with humble, meager beginnings is a long one. From tech startups to manufacturers to restaurants to service providers, they all have stories of people starting with little to nothing and building their little into something amazing. If you have a computer, tablet, or smartphone and internet connection then you have enough to at least start trying. You can start with a computer and a Wi-Fi connection. How much does that cost?

You can start a business out of your basement or garage. My wife has already done it three or four times. But when your business starts growing don't let it stall due to a lack of funding for expansion. Look into ways to obtain financing (home equity loan, business partners, start-up loan, etc..) that will allow you to continue the growth and expand operations. The "I'm too broke" insecurity will attempt to shift your focus from what you do have (skills, passions, uniqueness and any other resources on top of that) onto something you don't have (finances). Remember what I mentioned earlier? If you can develop your uniqueness into something with tangible value, then finances will follow. Whether the finances are through profits, partners willing to invest or banks wanting to support your vision. Value is always worth something. No matter how good or bad the economy is, value always attracts finances. The more you can build the value in your uniqueness, the less you will have to seek and worry about finances.

> "From tech startups to manufacturers to restaurants to service providers, they all have stories of people starting with little to nothing and building their little into something amazing."

Insecurity #4: What will other people think?

Response: This might be the toughest one of them all. This insecurity overemphasizes other people's opinions and underemphasizes our own internal opinion. But here's the truth, what other people think about you or your idea does not matter nearly as much as what you think about yourself or your idea. It's not even close. Self-belief leads to determination and perseverance. Determination and perseverance are pillars that lead to success. That isn't to say that we should not listen to others for ideas on improving or eliminating weaknesses. However, there is an ocean-sized difference between soliciting feedback from others as a tool for getting better and allowing other people's casual opinion to impose insecurity.

This is another insecurity which I have had to deal with while writing this book. *"What if everybody hates this? How will you handle the negative comments left on Facebook or Instagram? What if no one wants to publish it?"* This insecurity's goal is to train your mind to value other people's opinions more than your own opinions. This insecurity wants to demolish your own dreams based upon other people's flippant comments, real or make-believe.

Let's take it one step farther, how often do we entertain insecurity based upon our mere speculation of what other people would say? Think about it. Sometimes there is a real conversation made. Sometimes there is a real comment left on our Facebook wall. But how often are we writing scripts of speculative conversations in our head that may or may not ever happen? That's the shocking part. Sometimes the answer to the question, "What will everyone think of me?", is nothing. People probably won't think about you because they are intensely preoccupied with thinking about themselves. Most of our culture is so self-focused that they don't give other people the time of day. We must learn to revoke the influence other people have over our self-confidence. We must learn to establish an inner circle, people who love and care for us, who do have permission to give honest feedback and critiques. This is not to destroy us but it is for our benefit.

"Determination and perseverance are pillars that lead to success."

DO SOMETHING

As I review this list of common insecurities there is a definite common thread running through all of them. The common thread is this: Insecurity will often lead us to inaction or inappropriate action. Most people's actions fall into one of these two dangerous groups. Either their own internal insecurities lead them to take inappropriate and ill-advised action or it causes people to atrophy and take no action. Both results are harmful and are not going to lead us to move towards the intersection of our uniqueness.

Let's talk about the inappropriate action first. What do I mean by inappropriate action? These would be decisions we make which are primarily founded in a need to fill an insecurity. An example of this would be if we have an insecurity trying to convince us that we were not attractive. Someone might take that insecurity and try to fulfill the insecurity through the first relationship they could find. So instead of addressing the harmful thought process, someone would enter a relationship too quickly or too passionately. This would be an inappropriate action which could lead to a whole host of other issues. See what I mean? Inappropriate action isn't isolated just to relationships. We can take inappropriate action to prove something to someone else or even ourselves. We can start the wrong business, take the wrong job, or buy the wrong house or car. If our action is being fueled to eliminate an insecurity, then chances are it's the wrong thing to do. That's inappropriate action. Action which overcompensates for the insecurity inside of us.

The second bucket is people who take no action. Don't allow an insecurity to prevent you from moving forward. Instead, determine if the insecurity is based in an area of your life that is requiring some improvement or personal investment. If your insecurity says you're not experienced enough with running a kitchen to open a restaurant then instead of giving up, dig in. Get a job working in a kitchen to learn from someone who does have experience. Figure out a way to overcome insecurity with information, education, or self-investment. Those simple steps of becoming informed are steps of action. Researching a new business opportunity online, finding demographic information about the area you want to open a storefront, getting pre-approved for a start-up loan, these are all small steps in the process. But the important thing is that they are steps. From what I've learned with my own experiences and from other people is that as you take those first few steps you will begin to learn whether your idea is worth further investigation or effort. As you take those first few steps of action, you will discover the potential value of your idea.

Don't let insecurity of any kind keep you from fulfilling your destiny on Earth and arriving at your unique intersections. Instead of letting insecurity run in the background of your mind and covertly influence your actions and inactions, identify it today. Identify any insecurities that are commonplace in between your eyes and start handing out eviction notices. Inform your insecurity that it's going to have to find someone else to torment. Inform your insecurity that your relationship is over, and it must go!

CHAPTER 10 – THE HESITATION FACTOR

Have you ever seen two people who were very close, best friends even, and are convinced that they were basically the same person? Not that they looked the same, but they acted the same, they talked to same way, used the same slang words, and reacted to situations the same way. When I first met my wife in college, I remember thinking this about her and her best friend. They seemed to be the same person to me. Now, we had just met, and I had only interacted with her and her friend socially for a short time, but they were so very similar. So, so much. From an outside perspective they appeared to have a very similar personality. They liked the same kind of music. They liked to do the same kind of things for fun. They had the same major. They hung out with all the same people. They lived in the same room and wore similar styles of clothing. However, as I started to become friends with both, and got to know them both a lot better, the differences started to become a bit clearer. A lot clearer.

Hesitation and procrastination are kind of like that. Hesitation and procrastination are best friends. They are very similar but not completely identical. From a distance you might think they are indistinguishable, however, when you get up close and personal you see that they are a bit different. Both are damaging. Both like to put stuff off. Both like to trade doing something difficult today for something more enjoyable, or even doing nothing at all. Despite all their similarities there is a difference between the two of them that I'd like to address. Hesitation is more often the avoidance of internal focused changes while procrastination is more often the avoidance of external focused actions.

I hope that as you read through this chapter you can isolate your own tendencies to hesitate and procrastinate. Let's tackle them one-by-one.

HESITATION

When I was in high school my sport was soccer. I started playing it when I was four years old and got to be pretty good. Good enough, in fact, to be able to play in college. However, when I was a junior in high school, I was the only junior in my entire high school that played on the soccer team, so I recruited a few of my hockey-player friends to play soccer before hockey season started. It worked out great. They were able to stay in shape during the hockey off season and we got to hang out together on the soccer team. Everyone I recruited enjoyed playing soccer so much that most of them decided to play again for my senior year.

> "Hesitation is more often the avoidance of internal focused changes while procrastination is more often the avoidance of external focused actions."

Before our senior year soccer season started my friends said they would play under one stipulation. They told me that if I wanted them to play soccer again, then I had to play hockey. This was crazy. First, I'd never played hockey before. I used to go to free skates at the local ice rink in middle school on Friday nights for fun but that was about my extent of experience. Second, I owned no equipment. Zero. Zip. Just in case you didn't know, hockey equipment isn't exactly cheap. Well lucky for me, or not so lucky, one of my friends who was about my size was out for the entire season and couldn't play due to a shoulder injury. He gladly donated all his expensive, top of the line equipment to me for no cost just so he could watch me attempt to do this. I agreed. I would play hockey my senior year of high school.

Soccer season went great, well our team was awful, but we had fun together as friends. Sure enough, a few short week after soccer season ended, hockey season was just beginning. I practiced a bit when I could before the season officially began. I went to a few free skates and my friends tried to teach me some basic stick handling techniques, but I needed much more than a crash course in Hockey 101. I needed a full-scale hockey boot camp. Hockey season began and it went about as I expected. I was horrid. Here is the thing, I wasn't just horrid for an 18-year-old either, I was horrid for ages 14 and up.

Would you like to know the most humiliating part of this entire experience? Well, since my high school didn't have enough hockey players in tenth through twelfth grades, we had to play junior varsity hockey. What made matters worse was that in Pennsylvania eighth graders could play junior varsity if there was no middle school or ninth grade team. That meant I was potentially competing against 14-year-old boys and getting dominated. These little kids were skating around me like I had 50 lb. weights tied to my legs. They were better at stick handling and skating. Plus, they knew where to position themselves. It didn't matter if I was bigger and stronger because they were faster, more agile, and more skilled.

One of the more memorable moments of that season for me was this one particular game when I really confused my coach. Since my team had a bunch of seniors playing against freshmen and sophomores, we won a lot of games quite easily. This was great for me because I would get to play a lot at the end of the game when it didn't matter. It's called "garbage time". Garbage time is when all the garbage players get a chance for meaningless experience.

One game I was on the ice during garbage time (trying not to get leveled by a kid) and my teammate shot the puck into the offensive zone. I started skating as fast as I could, which wasn't very fast, to retrieve the puck. The other team beat me to the puck and changed the direction of the play. At this point I had to stop my momentum as quick as I could, turn around, and skate back the opposite way to play defense. Here was the problem, I only knew how to stop by turning in one direction which was by turning left. In this instance I was skating down the left side of the ice with the boards on my left. When the other team got the puck, I had to turn left into the boards, facing the crowd not the action.

Unbeknownst to me (because I was staring at plexiglass) my team stole the puck and my teammate passed it to me. Well, he actually passed the puck to where I should have been, which was right in front of the net, except I wasn't there. I didn't see the pass. I didn't see anything except some lady eating popcorn in the stands. My coach was none too happy. "BENEDETTI! Get off the ice, NOW!" I skated to the bench and began to try to explain what I was doing. "What do you mean you can't turn right? How can you play hockey and not be able to turn right?" I tried to tell him that was part of the problem. I'm not very good. I'm really quite bad at hockey.

What is the point in all of that? What is the point in my hockey abilities being limited to only stopping by turning in one direction? Here's the point, I had to turn away from the puck to function. I lost sight of the game because of my inability to perfect a skill. My hesitation to learn something new made me blind to the action. My hesitation to practice and work hard made me miss out on the play happening behind my back. My hesitation to directly and thoroughly confront my inabilities caused me to be ineffective.

The same principle applies to our self-improvement and advancing within a profession or our own business. The weaknesses or problems you have, when ignored, don't go away. In fact, those weaknesses tend to show themselves at the worst possible moments. If we want to operate at the highest output levels, we must stop hesitating and instead address our issues quickly and fully. Do not hesitate to be hard on yourself. Every insufficiency, issue or problem in your life has one, and only one, common denominator. YOU! I know that might be tough to read but it's the absolute truth. The longer you continue to refuse to ask yourself hard questions, the longer it will take to live in your full potential. You are in the middle of every relationship issue you have. You are in the middle of every workplace issue you have. You are in the middle of your financial issues you have. There is no getting around you.

> "If we want to operate at the highest output levels, we must stop hesitating and instead address our issues quickly and fully."

Now, here is the good news, and you must see it as good news, if you fix you then you fix your issues. If you fix one thing, then many things are instantly fixed. If you fix your patience, your kindness, and your love for other people, then you will experience the enormous ripple effect of internal change on all the circumstances surrounding you.

Do not allow hesitation to delay your advancement. Don't allow hesitation to stop you in your tracks. Think of my hockey analogy, hesitation to fix issues or failure to learn and grow will limit our vision in life. We won't be able to see clearly what is happening all around us because of our internal shortcomings. We will miss out on opportunities for growth because we failed to develop ourselves personally or as leaders. We will miss out on opportunities to expand because we hesitated to learn or develop a new skill. Don't hesitate to improve. Don't hesitate to change and develop. Don't miss out of success because you can't turn right.

PROCRASTINATION

There is a leadership author/speaker/motivator named Jocko Willink that I enjoy listening to. You might have heard of him or read some of his books such as *Extreme Ownership* or *The Dichotomy of Leadership*. I heard him describing his approach to procrastination in an interview. This former Navy Seal operator has a unique mindset when it comes to the temptation to procrastinate in his own life. His message was that he always procrastinates, but only with procrastination. He lives by the theory that anytime his mind tells him to procrastinate something, whether it is working out, writing a new book, or even household chores, he forces himself to do the action anyways and then he will take a break tomorrow if that feeling of procrastination comes back. This way of living works for him as it helps him maintain a high level of productivity while preventing him from burning out. He said that often the thought to procrastinate, or rest, seldom returns the next day. He said that if the feeling of exhaustion returns then he probably needs a mental or physical break from his heavy workload.

I like that mode of thinking. Only procrastinate with procrastination. Put off the act of putting things off. Procrastination is almost always associated with telling us not to do something worthwhile. Procrastination never seems to rear its ugly head when we want to take a nap or binge watch Netflix. The temptation for procrastination is almost a sign that should confirm we are on the right path. When our minds tell us to stop, don't work out, or stop being productive, it should trigger the thought, "Hey, this must be worth doing if my natural mind says to procrastinate."

> "Procrastination never seems to rear its ugly head when we want to take a nap or binge watch Netflix."

Personally, procrastination is a big one for me. Luckily my wife is not tempted at all by procrastination. Sometimes I have to hold her down and force her to relax. When we were newlyweds and didn't have enough money for cable television I would yell out, "FLOOR TIME" and wrestle her to the ground to talk and hear about her day. I did this because I noticed if I didn't mandate relaxation time, she would just clean and bake and plan and work all evening until her head would hit the pillow.

I have really taken to Jocko's method of procrastinating procrastination. Even as I was writing this book, I would often force myself to just write something each day. I would tell myself, "Just get out your laptop and do at least 100 words." Just keep the forward progress in motion. Keep moving forward. What I noticed is most nights, even if I just planned to write for 15 minutes, at least 40 minutes would pass, and I was still writing. Most nights when I forced myself to just write a little bit, maybe 200 words, I would write over 500 words. Like I said before, procrastination is more often the avoidance of external focused actions. What external actions have you been avoiding or ignoring? Don't procrastinate any longer. Take action and begin to see your life change for the better.

BAD INTENTIONS

Here is the goal of both hesitation and procrastination. They both intend for your today to resemble your yesterday. Here's the problem with that intention. If your yesterday wasn't propelling you towards your unique intersection, then your tomorrow will be the same as your today. If every day is like your yesterday, then every tomorrow will be the same as your today. Much like a house (or even my daughter's Batgirl Lego set) needs to be built with a plan, with intentionality, with patience, with a specific order, your life and future are also built with those things. You must take time out of your today to build your tomorrow. It's not just going to happen by accident. Don't put it off or schedule every day to be the same. Where will the difference come from? Where will the life change come from? Hesitation wants you to put off making self-improvements, not forever, but at least for this week or this month. Procrastination wants you to put off researching, studying, enrolling in a class or seminar, working on a product or developing a team around you because you are way too busy right now. Hesitation and procrastination will remind you that Rome wasn't built in a day so just relax a bit. You worked hard enough, leave it for tomorrow. It will be better tomorrow. Don't listen to those lies and that lazy mentality.

Every day is not created equally. Yes, everyday has 24 hours within it. We all are given the same 1,440 minutes each day and can decide how we spend each

> "You must take time out of your today to build your tomorrow."

one of them. However, every day is different with regards to the demands placed upon us those minutes. The demands on us, personally and professionally, differ from day-to-day. On some days my job is requesting, even demanding me to give more minutes towards it and away from something else. On some days my job doesn't just demand a few more minutes, it demands many, many, many more minutes. However, on the weekends my job demands very few and sometimes even zero minutes. My family has a request on my time every day and every week. Other life necessities place demands on our time. Our vehicles demand us to stop and fill up our gas tanks. Our stomachs demand us to take time to shop for groceries, prepare meals and eat. Our houses demand us to clean them, hopefully. Our clothes demand to be washed and cleaned, once again hopefully.

Then, there is another list of things that we want to give our minutes towards. These wouldn't be demands for our minutes, but things that we choose to give minutes towards. These are things like our faith, our churches, our family, our friends, our hobbies, and our work. Do you see how work is both a demand and a choice? Family is also both a demand and a choice. Here is what you must see in this whole set up, you are not an innocent bystander. Not at all. You are the steward or the manager handing out minutes to each of the areas placing demands on us. You are the steward handing out minutes to the areas based solely upon your own discretion. The demand areas and choice areas are both submitting order forms and we are managers of the distribution center of our daily 1,440 minutes deciding everyday which orders are to be filled, which orders go on backorder for tomorrow and which orders are ignored.

"Hesitation and procrastination will never demand minutes for your improvement or for productive actions."

Do you see how every day is not the same? Each day is different in some way. Certain days can be like others. For example, Mondays through Thursdays can look very similar, but they are never identical. For me, this is an empowering thought because it illustrates that I am always in control, even when it feels like I'm not. You might say that your boss dictates how your day goes. Your job dictates when you arrive and leave. However, you are still in control because you choose to go to work, this isn't communist Russia.

What does this have to do with hesitation and procrastination? Hesitation and procrastination will never demand minutes for your improvement or for productive actions. You have to delegate minutes out of your day, week, month, and year to overcome hesitation and procrastination.

TAKING BACK CONTROL

Take a minute to think a bit about your typical week. Think about your typical month. Think about the season of the year you are currently experiencing as you read this chapter (summer, winter, fall, or spring). Where do you see your time being wasted? Where do you see time you can redeem? There are seasons, quite literally seasons, that I am busier than others and busier in different areas. The fall is busy at the office because of our year ending on September 30th. The winter is typically the slowest season, after Christmas of course. The spring gets busy with my kids' soccer teams and yard work. The summer can be very busy at times with vacations, my golf obsession, and other fun activities. Then, it's fall again. The important consideration I have made is that, just as every day is different, each season of the year is different. I know that in the fall my pool of minutes available to be assigned to new demands is low. I know that in the winter my pool of minutes grows. In the summer I will have to make a choice between fun social activities or hobbies (mainly my golfing desires) and a new endeavor or investing in myself.

The main weapon that both hesitation and procrastination use to sabotage our progress is the weapon of excuses. Excuses are thieves, robbing us of a better tomorrow for the illusion of a more comfortable today. We make excuses as to why we can't do something hard, like enroll in a class online, and thus the excuse robs us of information. We make excuses as to why we couldn't take a risk, possibly because we don't have enough resource, and thus the excuse robs us of an opportunity. We make excuses as to why we shouldn't move forward today with action and progress on our goals, like because there's a lot of time and you deserve a nap, and thus a nap robs us of momentum.

> "Excuses are thieves, robbing us of a better tomorrow for the illusion of a more comfortable today."

Excuses aren't fully truthful all the time. In fact, excuses aren't truthful at all. Excuses will fill our heads with deception and half-truths. What excuses never explain is how each excuse we carry out compounds on top of one another. Excuses never explain that this compounding negative impact will multiply the length of time it will take to begin living in our unique intersection. Most people are aware of the effect of compounding interest. This means the longer you invest money the interest you earn on your investment begins to compound. After time, you are making money on your initial investment AND the interest already earned. This principle, when applied consistently over time won't just slowly grow your investment, it will begin to rapidly multiply. Think of hesitation and procrastination in the same way but with negative results which multiply with rapid effect when we entertain excuses. Inaction layered on inaction layered on inaction will set us back years. But the opposite is also true, action layered on progress layered on effort and dedication result in life change.

What do we do about the times and seasons when there are not a lot of extra minutes available to invest in ourselves or the pursuit of our uniqueness? Even if we are hesitating or procrastinating, how do we ensure consistent progress when life gets busy? Here's what you do, redeem your time. Stop wasting your time and instead redeem your time. You have to cut the grass, well listen to a podcast and redeem those minutes. You have to drive to work, well listen to interview on how someone in your desired field got started. This information is out there, available and FREE. You just have to access it. Start looking for ways to incorporate steps towards your intersection into your already existing routines and habits. If you work out regularly then use that time to listen to something. There are minutes all around you ready to be redeemed. Do you see them?

Redeem your time by making conscious choices not to procrastinate. Instead of watching another rerun on TBS, read a book. Instead of scrolling on Instagram for 45 minutes, improve a skill. Rome wasn't built in a day; it was built with a lot of consecutive days of action moving purposely towards the same goal. You may not arrive at your unique intersection in a day, it might take a bunch of days strung together where you decide this is a season for you to assign minutes to your future and your families future. Actions layered on actions.

CONCLUSION

It is my hope that this book has done a few things for you. I hope it has inspired you, informed you and challenged you. I hope it has motivated you to pursue the thing that makes you truly unique. I hope you stop defining yourself through your current occupation or status. I hope that you feel unlimited with what you can possibly do by just adding a '/' and adding to how you describe yourself.

This book was written, not out of desperation, but out of a strong desire to pursue a life I knew was waiting for my arrival. I like to think of it this way, have you ever been to the baggage claim at the airport and seen the drivers waiting for a passenger with their name on a sign? I remember when I was around 14 years old my whole family went to Walt Disney World for a week of vacation. When we arrived at Orlando Airport someone in my family noticed a man holding a sign that said, "Benedetti Family". Now, 'Benedetti' isn't exactly a common last name, so we suspected when we saw the sign that the driver was for us. My dad walked over to the driver and began to ask some questions to see if he was there to take us to our hotel. Little did we know that due to shortages of the standard vans supposed to take us to our resort Disney had orchestrated to have a limousine pick us up instead. For some reason my mom and dad didn't even know about the complimentary upgrade. Our travel agent didn't even know about the change. Good thing one of us noticed the man holding his little whiteboard and good thing our last name is so unique. What a great surprise that was for everyone. We thought it was just going to be an ordinary thirty-minute commute instead it was a thirty-minute joy ride I will never forget.

Consider this book like a man in a suit holding a sign with your name on it ready to take you on a ride. Here's the difference though, this ride doesn't take you to the same place you were planning on going. This ride will take you to a place even better than you could have planned. It would have been like that limousine driving past the hotel my parents booked and going straight to the Ritz Carlton or Four Seasons. Now, just because the destination is far better than we would have hoped doesn't mean it will be easy. Fulfilling purpose rarely is easy, but I'm sure it will be memorable and well worth your effort.

As I mentioned above, I hope this book has informed you. I expect that, as you read this, you learned about the possibility of a future you had never thought about. I trust you have gleaned some practical steps to begin discovering how you can engage this new future. I am confident that you have now learned and identified about your skills, your passions and found unique ways by which your skills intersect with your passions. I believe that you have learned how to determine the potential value within each intersection to know in which direction to begin moving. I am trusting that you have been encouraged to overcome fear, hesitations and insecurities which will try their best to impede your progress. I'd like to end this book with some simple reminders and encouragement.

First, don't let this book die in the space of your mind or on the paper you wrote your lists of skills, passions, and intersections. Don't let your inspiration fizzle out and don't let the information fade away. Inspiration is like a fire. The work that it took to prepare and build a roaring fire will not keep the fire going and going forever. Meaning, we must keep feeding the fire of inspiration even long after the fire was initially started.

MAINTAIN YOUR MOTIVATION

So, how do we maintain inspiration and motivation, especially in times when we don't feel especially motivated or very inspired? There must be a motive fueling your motivation which is deep enough, and strong enough, to last year-after-year. It must last late at night and early in the morning. It has to last when situations may not go in your favor. It must last when other people disappoint you, let you down, or fail you. I would advise this, don't let your motivation or inspiration be result driven. Meaning this, if your motivation is to provide a certain level of income so your family is financially comfortable, or so you can pay for your children's college tuition, then your motivation ends once your goal is achieved. A financial motivation is fleeting and never truly fulfilling. If your motivation is to open a business, then how will you stay inspired to run and operate the business?

Your motivation should be directly tied to your destiny. My motivation is to do something that gives me the feeling of purpose. My inspiration is to be able to help other people discover their own uniqueness so they can fulfill their dreams.

> "There must be a motive fueling your motivation which is deep enough, and strong enough, to last year-after-year."

Those motivations can't be checked off a to-do list. There is permanence to them. This inspiration will long be motivating me after writing this book. This motivation will be urging me to take additional steps towards living in my uniqueness.

Finding your true inspiration and motivation will keep the fire of drive roaring in your life. During times of weariness or stress, relying on these inspirational factors will motivate me to keep working and keep pushing ahead. Keep the fire going. Whether its chopping wood or tending to the logs already burning, it takes continual focus and attention. There are easy, practical ways to ensure your motivation doesn't burn out. Create pictures of what motivates you and put the pictures in a place where you can regularly see them. These are commonly called vision boards. Take a simple cork board and start pinning up pictures of the goals you have for yourself. If you can devote a minute each day to look at your board, it will have the effect of adding a log or two onto the fire each day.

NEVER QUIT

Second, I'd like to encourage each person reading this to not give up even if things aren't looking like you planned. How do we maintain inspiration and motivation even when it seems like nothing is working out and things aren't going our way? Jimmy Valvano, a former collegiate basketball coach, famously said, "Don't give up. Don't ever give up". I love the simplicity and power within that quote. Don't give up if it seems like you are not making progress. Don't give up if a decision doesn't go your way. Don't give up if it appears like your door of opportunity is shutting or was slammed closed in your face.

I learned a little bit about the process of climbing Mt. Everest that I found interesting. See, climbing Mt. Everest isn't like taking a weekend hike at a local trail. Climbing the tallest peak on Earth takes months of preparation, tens of thousands of dollars, and weeks of actual ascending, slowly and carefully, towards the peak. The Everest climb is not for the faint of heart and it's not for the faint of wallet either. I always assumed that the process of climbing to the altitude of 29,029 feet was slow and steady, but the actual climbing agenda shocked me when I read about it. When I mean the climbing agenda, I mean the day-in, day-out plan to climb to the top in a way that gives climbers the best chance for reaching the summit. (In interest of full disclosure, upon my own research into climbing Mt. Everest I found that there are multiple routes and methods. What I am about to describe is one particular method as experienced by the author of the article I read.)

"Don't give up if it seems like you are not making progress. Don't give up if a decision doesn't go your way. Don't give up if it appears like your door of opportunity is shutting or was slammed closed in your face."

The Mt. Everest ascent starts at base camp and there are three additional camps higher and higher up the mountain on this route. The climb is structured this way in order to allow the climber's bodies to acclimate to the drastic altitude change they were experiencing with each trek to the next camp. I always assumed that the adventurers would progress from the Base Camp to Camp 1 and spend a few days at Camp 1 to get used to the higher altitude. Then, they would climb to Camp 2 and spend a few days there. Next, they would climb to Camp 3 and after a few days at Camp 3 the climbers would then attempt to reach Mt. Everest's summit. Well, this assumption was dead wrong. I couldn't believe what I learned, and the principals contained within the process of the dangerous climb. Forget my wrong assumption I just mentioned, this is the reality that climbers actually faced:

Step 1 - They climb from Base Camp to Camp 1 and spend a few days at Camp 1 so their bodies can adjust to functioning at the higher altitude. But then they descend back down the mountain to Base Camp because staying at that altitude permanently would cause illness.

Step 2 - Then, from Base Camp they climb to Camp 1. They spend a few days at Camp 1, then ascend to Camp 2. They spend a few days at Camp 2 to adjust as well but then trek all the way back down to Base Camp, passing Camp 1.

Step 3 - Next, they climb from Base Camp to Camp 1 and stay at Camp 1 for a few days. Then, they ascend from Camp 1 to Camp 2 and spend a few more days at Camp 2. Then, they climb all the way up to Camp 3, the last camp before attempting to reach the peak. They spend a few days at Camp 3 adjusting further but then, almost tragically, they painstakingly have to turn their back on the prize and begin descending back down to Camp 2, then Camp 1, and ultimately all the way back down to the beginning at the Base Camp.

Step 4 - Then, finally, the summit push. The climbers repeat the same process they had been doing for weeks. Climb to Camp 1, wait and adjust to the altitude. Climb to Camp 2, wait and adjust to the altitude. Climb to Camp 3, wait and adjust to the altitude. Then, finally climb to the top of Mount Everest at 29,029 feet.

I learned through some research online that Camp 3 is only about 1 mile from the summit. After already climbing about 15 total miles, I can't imagine how mentally difficult it must be to essentially be starting from the beginning after getting so close to the top of the mountain. I can't imagine how frustrating that must be, to be so close in proximity from your goal, and yet to have to turn around and walk back down to the same point where you started from.

WHAT'S THE POINT?

Here is the principal that we can apply from the Mt. Everest climb, steps that were taken moving the climber away from the peak were still steps taken moving the climber towards the peak. Steps going down the mountain are actually steps towards the top. "Wait, what? That doesn't make any sense." These could be your internal thoughts right now. Let me clarify, if you view progress only as movement up the mountain then it indicates a level of ignorance in the process of reaching the ultimate goal. The process of the climb is structured in a way to give the best chance of success. As such, the process dictates that moving away from the peak is just as valuable, important and productive as walking towards the peak. Why? If someone were to only climb higher and higher each day, if someone were to ignore the advice, counsel, and wisdom of others and climb as high as they could as fast as they could then that person would most likely die en route.

The process of climbing up and down, up and down, up and down has purpose and intentionality. The purpose is for safety and the intention is to produce the highest chance for a successful result. The people who were able to achieve success in their goal to climb Mt. Everest were able to see each step as a step towards the goal, regardless of the direction or the elevation being changed by each step. Walking down the mountain is still getting you closer to the summit even though it seems like you are going in the wrong direction.

> "The people who were able to achieve success in their goal to climb Mt. Everest were able to see each step as a step towards the goal, regardless of the direction or the elevation being changed by each step."

PROGRESS VS. PROCESS

There might be moments in your adventure of climbing towards your goal that seem to be contrary to progress. Remember this, progress and process are not always the same. If you understand that inside the process of becoming or building something successful are steps that seem backwards, then you will be reassured to keep moving and fighting to realize your full potential. Progress insists that every step is forward, and everything works out the way you planned. However, a process allows for situations that seem to be going in reverse, so that we can adjust our attitude, learn something new, develop as a leader, or improve a skill so we can go even higher the next time.

The point of the climbing up and down the mountain so many times isn't to simply frustrate people or make it seem more difficult than it already is. The point isn't to "really let the climbers get their money's worth out of the experience." The point of the process is for the climber's safety and to ensure they can succeed the higher they go.

The Bible talks about this same principle in Matthew 25 with the parable of the talents. The parable teaches that a wealthy man gave out talents to three of his servants, or stewards. Each steward is responsible for managing what he had been given. Each steward was given different levels of talents that they were to manage and oversee. Two of the stewards were able to double the talents given to them while the third steward lazily hid his money in the ground. When the master returned, he called a meeting with his stewards to find out what they had done with the level of talents they were given. Upon the steward's own reports, the master commended the two stewards who doubled their money by saying, "Well done my good and faithful servant. You have been faithful with a few things; I will put you in charge of many things." The third steward however wasn't commended or complimented. In fact, he was harshly scolded for not managing properly what he had been given. Even though he didn't lose the money, he also didn't use his own abilities to work with the talent (money) he had been given.

See, the master had to ensure that the steward had the ability to manage and succeed with a smaller portion before a steward could be given more responsibility. If the steward couldn't handle the pressure of the small amount he had been given, then he certainly could not have handled any more.

The hard truth from this principle is that you are managing exactly the amount you can handle. You are where you are because of what you have done with what you were given. I am where I am with my finances because of how I've managed money thus far. This parable is a bit intimidating for me because it gives no allowance for excuses in our lives. The parable tells me that I will be given the promotion when I'm able to handle the position. The parable tells me that my team will succeed when I learn how to manage and inspire better. This tells me that my marriage will improve when I learn how to love more completely and rid myself of selfishness. Excuses are out the window.

> "I hope you see through this book that you have been given something. You have been given talents, abilities, skills and passions."

WHAT HAVE YOU BEEN GIVEN?

I hope you see through this book that you have been given something. You have been given talents, abilities, skills and passions. However, it is up to you to prove your faithfulness with what you have, and then you will create the capacity and ability to manage more. Climbers must prove they can advance to Camp 2 by showing they can climb to Camp 1. The higher you want to climb, the harder you are required to train. The higher you want to successfully ascend at life, the more diligently you have to invest in yourself and your uniqueness.

Do you remember in the introduction how I mentioned the nation of Israel traveling in the desert, on the way to their destiny in the Promised Land? The same traveler's fatigue that plagued the Israelite people is the same traveler's fatigue that will attempt to delay your arrival at your destiny. Do not allow, but refuse and reject, an attitude of complaining to overtake your mind and emotions. Refuse to allow impatience to stop your progress. The Apostle Paul wrote in Galatians 6:9, "So let's not get tired of doing what is good. At just the right time we will reap a harvest of blessing if we don't give up." What the Apostle Paul was saying was, "Don't give up! Don't stop because you don't know how close you are to your breakthrough." The Israelites' attitude lengthened their travel time passing through the desert from 11 days to 40 years. Even when it seems like you are not making progress, or it even seems like you are losing ground, know this: Each step is a step towards your purpose, your destiny, and your success.

Thomas Edison had 1,000 failed experiments before inventing the lightbulb. Each unsuccessful try was one step closer to changing the world. Sylvester Stallone's script of Rocky was rejected over 1,500 times by movie producers. Each rejection was one step closer to winning an Oscar. The list of those who overcame an incredible amount of rejection goes on and on.

I'm learning, both from observation within myself and from other successful leaders and entrepreneurs, that there is a dichotomy of growth. Once you start the process you will realize that there really isn't an "end". There is a definite starting line to our leadership journey, however, especially for people striving to fulfill purpose not just fund a 401(k), there is only the illusion of a finish line. True leaders never stop growing. John Maxwell is 72 years old (as of early 2019). He just released his most recent book, *Leadershift: The 11 Essential Changes Every Leader Must Embrace*, only weeks before he celebrated his 72nd birthday. Per Wikipedia this new book, *Leadershift*, is the 68th book he's written. 68 books! What, are you kidding me? At some point, after finishing and publishing book #65, he must have thought, "Nope, there's still more I can contribute. There's still more I can teach and pass on to other people."

> "No matter where you are at in the cycle of life, never stop looking to grow."

It's amazing what limitations people will put on themselves. I'm too young. I'm too old. I'm too _____, fill in the blank. Mr. Maxwell illustrates perfectly that the unlimited life is only lived by those who have removed all limits. His age isn't a lid that limits his capabilities. His age is an attribute that only increases his value and output. The longer he lives the more he learns. The more he learns, the more he grows. The more he grows, the more he can impart and grow others. It's a vicious cycle of output.

No matter where you are at in the cycle of life, never stop looking to grow. Never stop looking to develop. Never stop looking to contribute and provide value, either to yourself or more importantly, to other people. Benjamin Franklin once said, "Nothing can be said to be certain, except death and taxes." I suppose there is a finish line to our growth, the moment we breathe our last breath on this Earth. What you do between this moment and crossing that finish line is up to you.

Embrace being multidimensional. Embrace the '/' by allowing the slash to describe you, not define you. You don't have to just be one thing or have just one focus. You can be this and that. You can do many things successfully, not just one.

You are uniquely skilled.

You are uniquely passionate.

Your future and destiny await your arrival at the intersection of your skills and your passions.

Don't make your full potential wait long, get going, and get after it. I can't wait to see what you can do.

Made in the USA
Monee, IL
07 March 2021